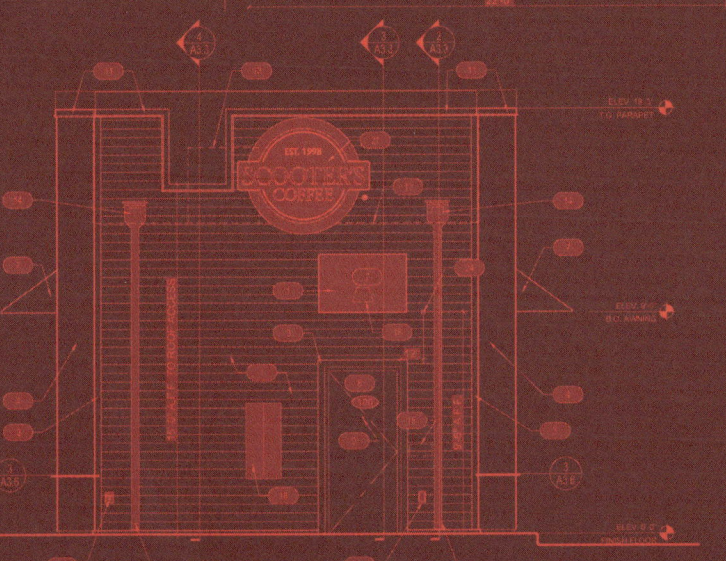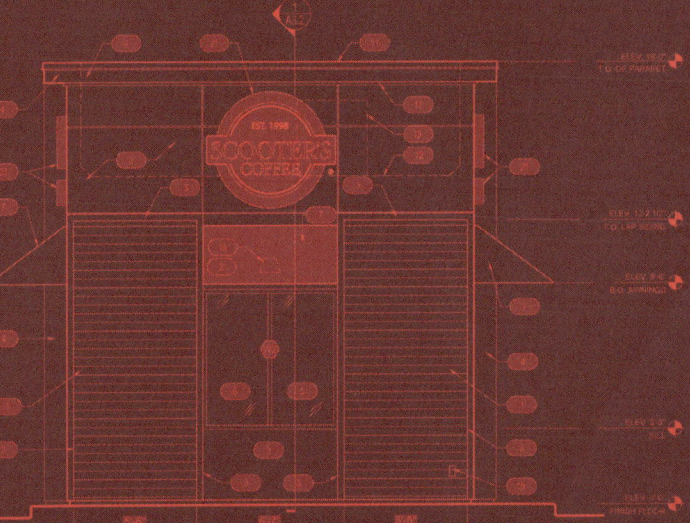

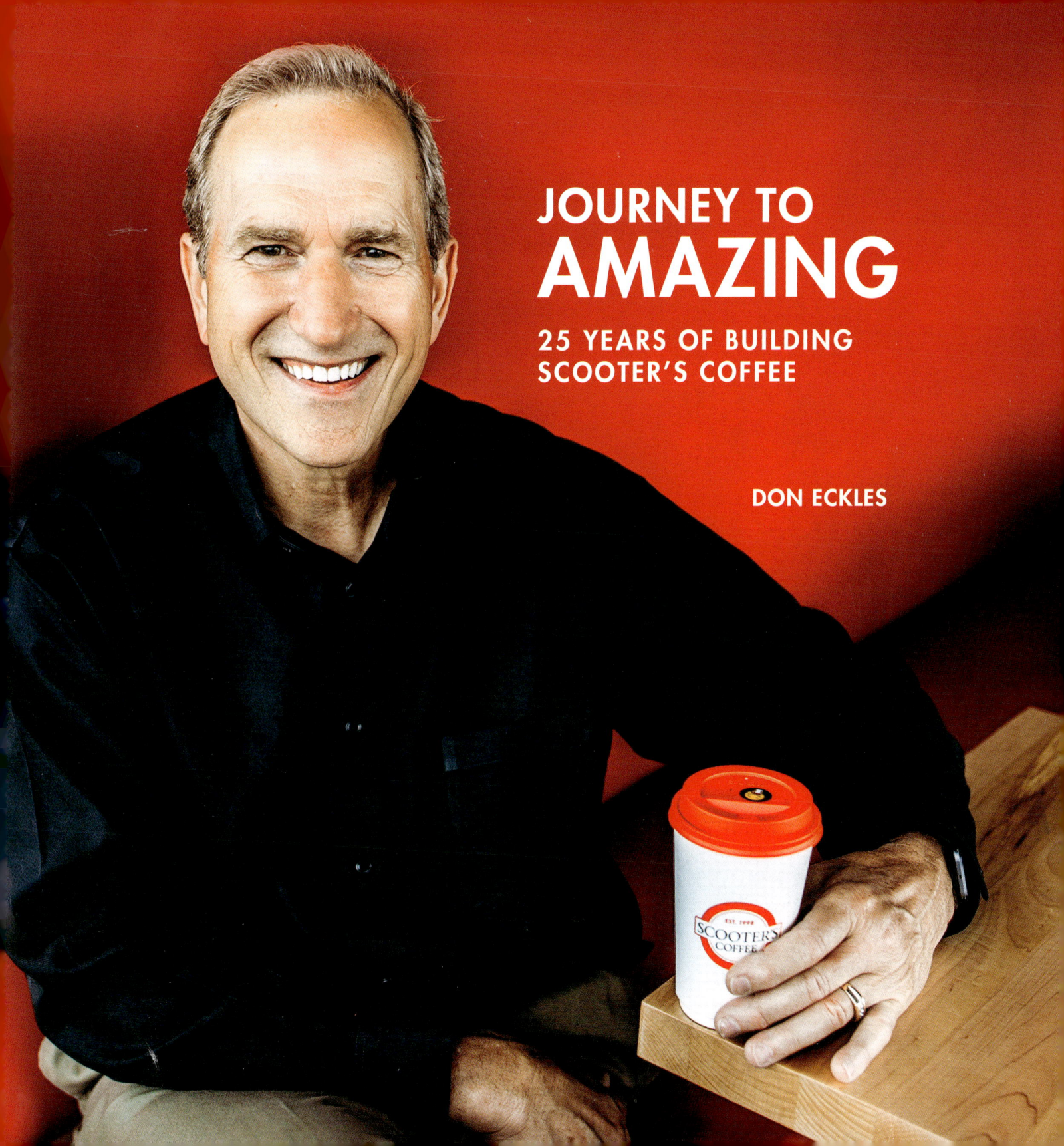

JOURNEY TO AMAZING
25 YEARS OF BUILDING SCOOTER'S COFFEE

BY DON ECKLES

EDITOR AND REPORTER
Steve Jordon

DESIGNER
Christine Zueck-Watkins

*On the back cover:
Traci Gabriel,
Don and Linda Eckles
and Chandra Kipper.*

Copyright © 2023
Scooter's Coffee.
All rights reserved.

No part of this book may be reproduced, stored in a retrieval system, or transmitted in any form or by any means, electronic, mechanical, photocopying, recording or otherwise, without prior consent of the publisher, Scooter's Coffee.

Scooter's Coffee
11808 Miracle Hills Dr.
Omaha, NE 68154
scooterscoffee.com

First Edition
ISBN: 979-8-218-14231-5

Printed by
Walsworth Publishing Co.

16	**INTRODUCTION** TAKING A STEP BACK
22	**CHAPTER 1** STRUGGLES IN SCHOOL
30	**CHAPTER 2** GETTING JOBS
34	**CHAPTER 3** RACING THE IDITAROD
40	**CHAPTER 4** IOWA, AGAIN
42	**CHAPTER 5** CALIFORNIA, HERE WE GO
44	**CHAPTER 6** JAVA? WHAT'S THAT?
50	**CHAPTER 7** COMING HOME
56	**CHAPTER 8** COFFEE TO GO
68	**CHAPTER 9** GROWTH BY FRANCHISING
88	**CHAPTER 10** HARVEST ROASTING
104	**CHAPTER 11** A NEW EXECUTIVE TEAM
114	**CHAPTER 12** ZIG-ZAGGING
124	**CHAPTER 13** THE FUTURE
138	**INDEX**

WELCOME!

Linda and I greeted our first Scooter's Coffee customers in 1998, beginning an amazing journey that celebrates 25 years in 2023.

In these pages, you'll learn how our business grew from one location in Bellevue, Nebraska, into one of the nation's largest drive-thru coffee chains. Scooter's Coffee's success is built on great locations, high-quality drinks, speed of service and a BIG smile — our Core Competency:

WE DELIVER HIGH-QUALITY, HIGH-MARGIN DRINKS THROUGH A DRIVE-THRU LANE, FAST AND FRIENDLY.

We're supported by dynamic business principles and four strong Core Values: Integrity, LOVE, Humility and Courage.

— DON ECKLES

INTEGRITY. LOVE. HUMILITY. COURAGE.

We've built our company around these core values because that's the way we want to live our lives, and people who share those values are the kind of people we want to be around. Ironically, it's resulted in us being able to attract great employees and franchisees — a side benefit. We didn't create the core values to attract people necessarily, but that's been the result. We created them to help us define who we are and want to be as a company. It turns out, not so surprisingly, that others want to be a part of that, too.

Within the walls of our company we focus on two things: our core values and profitability at the store level. Our core values because that's who we want to be, and profitability at the store level because our franchisees have invested in their dream and in our company. In many cases they've invested their life savings. They're trusting us to get it right.

As we hire employees, we make sure they know how important those two things are to us. We want to be a world-class franchisor and a world-class employer. Being the second makes it easier to be the first. Great employers attract great people, and great people accomplish great things.

Finally, we recruit to our core values. Core values are the beginning and the end of every recruiting conversation. We want to pay really well, but never the most. Why? We believe that if people come to you for the money, they'll leave you for more money. There has to be more to it than money. That's where the culture and core values come in. I've learned over the years that if you like what you do, and you like who you do it with, and you make a good living, that's as good as it gets. We try very hard to be the kind of company that's hard to leave. ●

CORE VALUE

INTEGRITY

We uphold the highest moral and ethical principles. Everything we do is built on a foundation of honesty and trust. We say what we mean and we mean what we say.

We require integrity of everyone we work with — each other, employees, franchisees, vendors, lenders, everyone. Trust is the basis of any good relationship, and if you don't have integrity, you'll never have trust. If you lack integrity, you can't stay here. That's just the way it is.

CORE VALUE

LOVE

We approach one another with kindness, respect and grace. We actively listen and show empathy with a caring, understanding heart.

We often show LOVE as larger than the others because love should be at our very core. It should be the lens through which we view every situation with people. Compassion, caring and empathy are all things we should embrace. Giving people the benefit of the doubt is a good place to start. That doesn't mean that no one is held accountable for results or their actions, but it does mean that not everything is always black and white. Usually if you have two people with goodwill, a solution can be found.

LOVE

CORE VALUE

HUMILITY

We seek to build up others, not ourselves. We acknowledge and celebrate each other's accomplishments because we know we can't truly succeed on our own.

None of us is "all that." The most attractive and interesting people to me are people who really are a big deal, but either don't know it or don't believe it. It's hard to take people seriously when they are taking themselves seriously enough for both of us. The reverse is also true: Arrogance is very unattractive. High achievers are generally very confident, either naturally or as a result of a learned behavior. Confidence is a good thing. Arrogance is not.

HUMILITY

CORE VALUE

COURAGE

We embrace challenges and encourage new ideas. We have the curiosity to ask questions, to continue learning, and to explore new possibilities.

Courage isn't about putting up your dukes. It's about doing the right thing even when you're the only one who does. Or maybe it's about offering ideas that may get rejected. Or maybe it's reporting a behavior that doesn't seem right, even if the offender is a high-level person. It might be stepping outside your comfort zone to try new things. Doing the right thing takes courage sometimes. But doing the right thing is always the right thing to do, regardless of the consequences.

INTRODUCTION

TAKING A STEP BACK
LEARNING FROM MISTAKES

ALTHOUGH LINDA AND I started Scooter's Coffee, many others deserve credit for the fact that soon we will have 1,000 stores across the nation and the potential to multiply that number in years to come.

Don and Linda operate a coffee cart, a feature of Sweet Things & Java, at a soccer match in the Sacramento area. "In the morning it would be chilly, on a California scale, and we'd sell a ton of coffee," Don said.

Journey to Amazing explores the history, the people and the secrets of Scooter's Coffee. I'm also excited to share lessons I've learned along the way, some painful and some heartening, that may be valuable to you, whether in business or simply in life.

I've failed at many things. I've never taken bankruptcy, but I've lost all my money too many times to count. One of those lessons, which I believe is important for everyone to learn, helped me stop failing: Learning the difference between mere obstacles and real closed doors.

If we see every obstacle as a closed door, we won't accomplish many big things, because accomplishing big things is hard by itself. You can bet there will be lots of obstacles along the way. An obstacle might be a bank telling you "no." A closed door is every bank telling you "no." We need to be able to tell the difference.

As a young, aggressive guy, I used to think you have to find a way. I didn't have anybody putting their arm around me saying, "No, Don, slow down, use your noodle here a little bit and think things through a little better."

OUR MISSION IS TO CREATE AN AMAZING EXPERIENCE FOR EACH LIFE WE TOUCH.

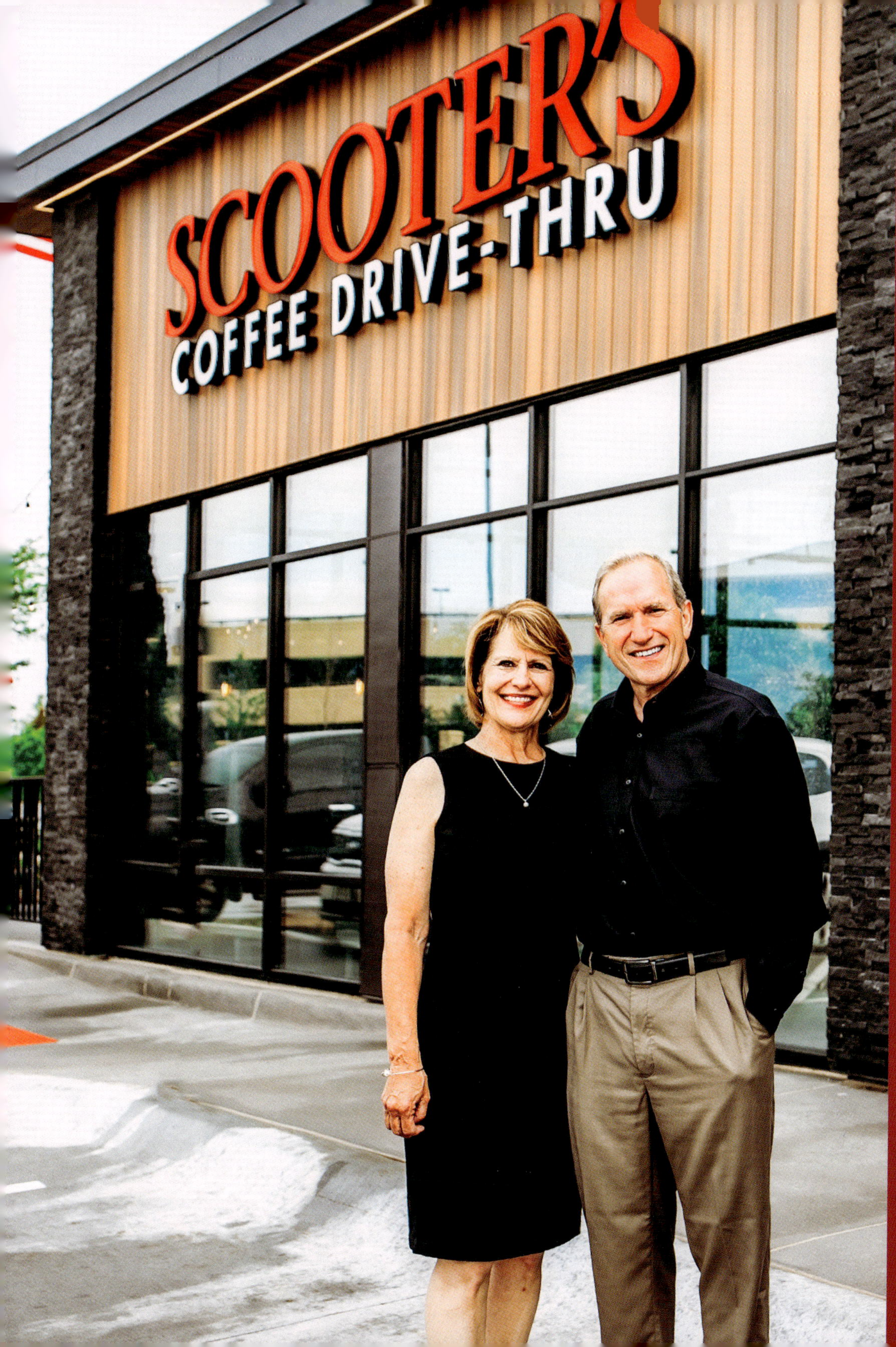

CO-FOUNDERS
DON & LINDA ECKLES

We developed the concept of "Be Amazing" because we believe that everyone has something about them that is special ... even amazing. They just may not know it. We, as leaders, have the opportunity to help people find that part of themselves that's special.

LESSONS LEARNED

Acquiring wealth takes time. You've probably never heard that one before, but it's as basic as basic gets. There is no free lunch. Nobody is going to give it to you (whatever "it" is). You can have virtually anything in life, as long as you don't have to have it today and you're willing to work for it.

If a door would close — I couldn't get financing from a bank, for example — I'd go to another bank and another bank and another bank. After a series of "no's," I might borrow money from family or friends, or mortgage my home or car, or whatever I needed to finance my "can't miss" idea. As an aggressive young businessman, I just kicked the doors down.

I eventually figured out that closed doors are, in my opinion, God saying, "Don't do it, Don. Not a good idea."

When I stopped kicking the doors down, I started stepping back and saying, "Why are these doors closed?" If banks aren't wanting to lend me money, maybe I ought to stop and think about why. Banks make money by lending out money, but only if they get it back with interest. Landlords want to lease space, but they want tenants who are going to be good for their property and who are going to pay the rent.

Maybe they don't think what I'm about to do is going to work. Maybe I ought to rethink my idea a little bit. Maybe that idea isn't as good as I think it is. Or maybe it is, but I need to flesh out the idea better.

Same thing for hiring and keeping good people. If someone is going to leave, it's too late to save them. Most people check out long before they leave. Checking back in is almost impossible. At that point, I need to figure out where I lost them, and try not to make that mistake again.

Whether you believe it's God closing the door or just people smarter than you who don't believe your plan will work, closed doors should be an opportunity to step back and rethink things a bit.

The amazing story of Scooter's Coffee is a chance for you to step back and gain insights that may open doors and help you avoid some of my past mistakes. In any case, please enjoy this account of a business created, and thus far succeeding, in the best tradition of American entrepreneurship.

Don Eckles, Chairman of Scooter's Coffee

OUR BRAND PROMISE | AMAZING PEOPLE, AMAZING DRINKS ... AMAZINGLY FAST!®

CARAMELICIOUS
OUR SIGNATURE DRINK

SMILEY STICKERS
ON EVERY LID SINCE 1998

FIRST SCOOTER'S COFFEE
BELLEVUE, NE
HEADQUARTERS
OMAHA, NE

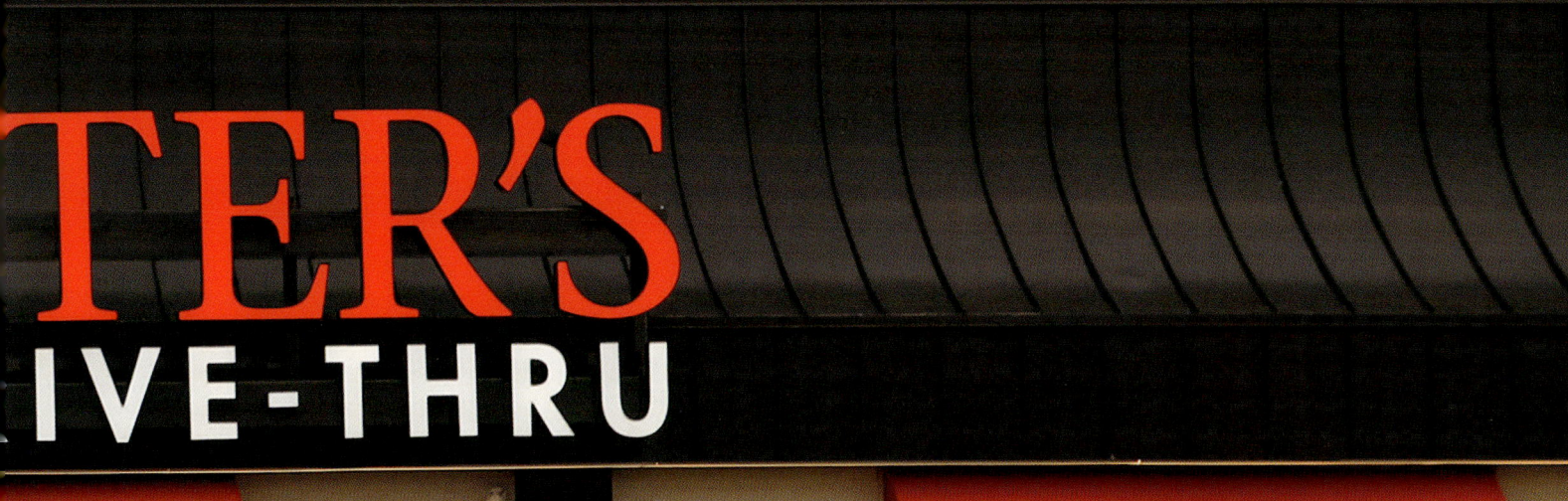

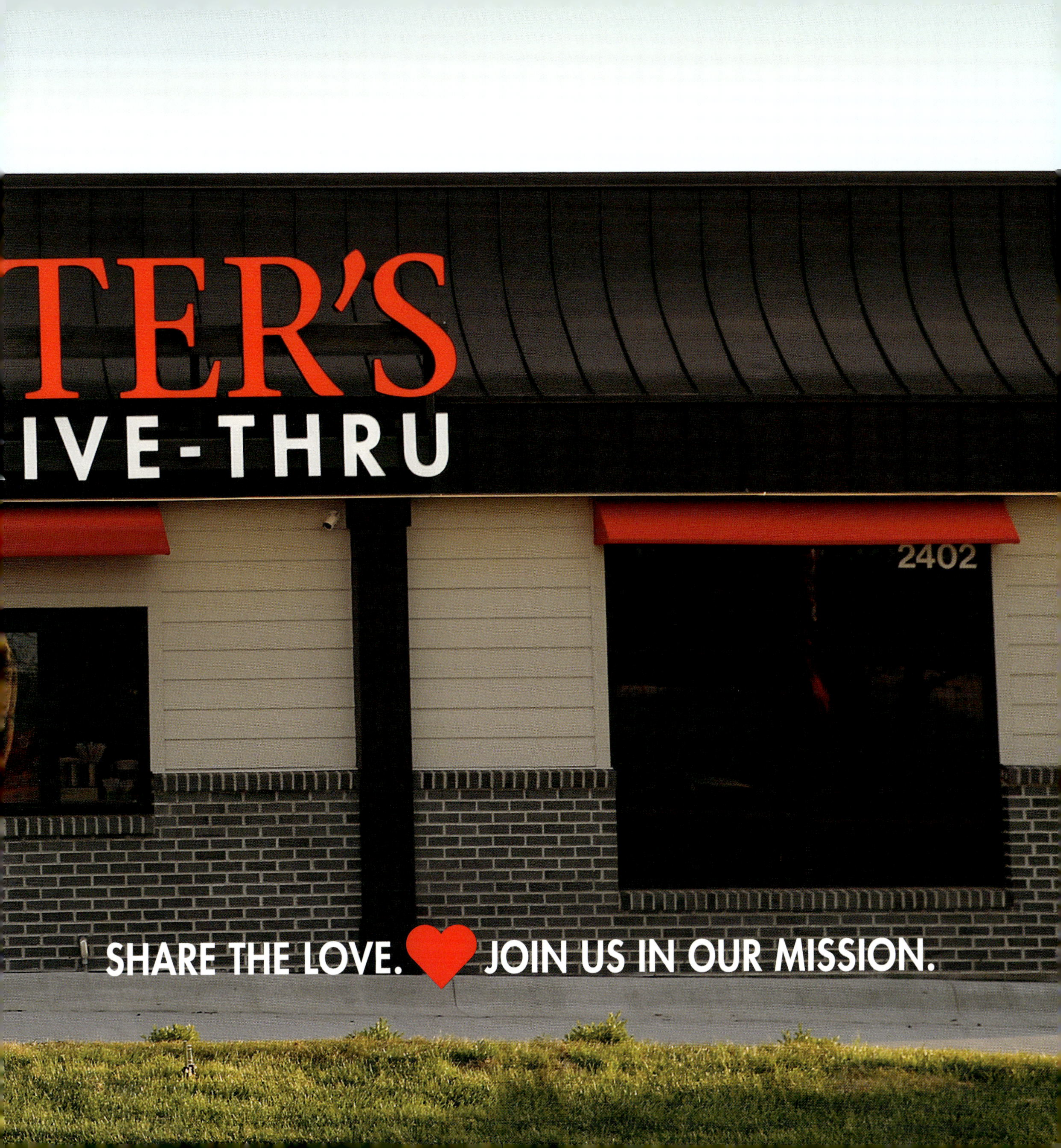
TER'S
IVE-THRU
2402
SHARE THE LOVE. JOIN US IN OUR MISSION.

CHAPTER 1

STRUGGLES IN SCHOOL
RADIO LEADS TO ROMANCE

OUR FAMILY LIVED IN Omaha's Westgate area, a middle-class neighborhood that was on the southwestern edge of Omaha and now is somewhere in the middle. Dad was a Greyhound bus driver, and Mom worked as a cook at Valley View Junior High, making $15 a day. That was a great job because she was home with us when school was out.

"I was the odd one in the family. My dad just didn't understand me."

— DON ECKLES

We were working class. I went to Westside High School with kids whose fathers were in Congress, or who owned car dealerships or department stores. I went to the "rich kids" school and wasn't a rich kid. While I had a lot of friends, my perception at that time was that my whole life seemed to be about not fitting in.

I did have parents who loved me, but because of the nature of my dad's job he was gone half the time. He was a union member who lost his job when Greyhound members went out on strike not long before he was supposed to retire. He had to work as an over-the-road trucker the last few years of his working life. He eventually got his Greyhound pension, but it was less.

Don, age 2, at his grandparents' farm near Winterset and Greenfield, Iowa.

 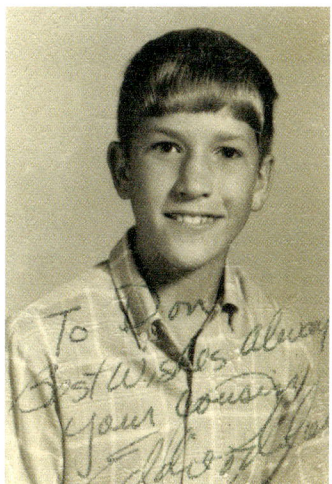

Top, left: Don at age 6 and his mother in Cedar Rapids, Iowa, where the family lived until they moved to Omaha before 4th grade. Top, right: Wayne and Myrna Eckles sent their son's 7th grade class photo for an autograph to a cousin who played football for the University of Iowa and the Kansas City Chiefs. The inscription: "Best wishes always. Your cousin, Ed Podolak."

Don (No. 3 in the back row) played for Wilson Concrete's Little League team in Omaha's Westgate neighborhood, with coaches Ray Lampe, left, and Ted Melonis, right.

GOOD GRIEF

Every now and then I'll give a talk in a high school class or a business class at college or a small group and I'll tell people when I was growing up, I wasn't sure if my last name was Eckles or Good Grief, because all I ever heard from my dad was, "Don, good grief."

— DON ECKLES

When I was in high school, I was a very poor student. I knew college wasn't in the cards for me, but I was intrigued by radio. There was a disc jockey over at KOIL Radio named Jim Fox who was the evening guy. A few years later he became Eric Fox at WOW Radio. Sometimes he would let me come into the station and watch him do his thing. I knew I wanted to be in radio.

My backyard neighbor was Dale Munson, a well-known TV and radio personality in Omaha. Dale had attended the Brown Institute of Broadcasting in Minneapolis and suggested that might be a place for me to start.

In high school, if there were 870 kids in my class, I was looking at the bottom of the shoes of 865 of them. I just was a complete screw-up, a goof-off in school.

I did well in things I liked, speech and English and things like that, but geometry? Seriously, what is geometry?

Don's high school senior photo. He graduated from Westside High School in 1973.

As I reflect on my time there, I see a kid who was basically a good kid, but lost. My parents, who loved me, weren't equipped to help me develop as a young man. They tried their best to keep me in line, but the truth is, we all are victims of our environment. We only know what we've seen or done or have been able to figure out on our own.

Looking back, I see a kid who did poorly in high school and consequently graduated thinking he was not very bright. Many teachers, but not all, didn't waste a ton of time on a kid who didn't seem to care. I wasn't unpopular, but I wasn't popular, either. I was just kind of invisible. I suspect that there are more kids who feel like that than not.

There's also a false sense of reality in high school that I don't think we ever really contemplate. No matter what your background, or how rich or poor your parents are, high schoolers basically live the same life. We eat the same food in the same cafeteria. We wear the same gym clothes and participate in the same activities. Once you graduate from high school, that all stops. If you want to have things, you have to work for them. The sooner we understand that, the better.

LESSONS LEARNED

I have empathy for other people because I realize that most of us are screwballs in high school. We don't know who we are. You're kind of finding your way, unless you've got a really strong presence in your life to put their arm around you and kind of guide you a little bit.

College was never even discussed in my family. I barely graduated from high school. Neither I nor my parents had any thought of my continuing down the four-year education path. We couldn't have afforded it even if I had wanted to go to college. Student loans were an unfamiliar concept to us.

To attend Brown Institute (later Brown College), I worked a part-time job and borrowed money from my younger, more responsible brother. My parents paid my rent and utilities, which had to be a stretch for them.

I loved it there and began to think that maybe I wasn't as dumb as I thought. I loved the classes and graduated with a B-plus GPA. I often joke that I couldn't spell B-plus when I was in high school. Several years removed from high school, I began to realize that it wasn't that I was dumb, it's that I wasn't interested. When I found something that interested me, I was actually fairly good at it.

That awareness has given me a heart for kids. We live in what must be confusing times for kids. And through my own experiences I realize that many, maybe even most, kids don't have the self-awareness or the guidance they need to find their own correct path.

Just as my family was not familiar with student loans, many kids and their families have no idea how to change their future for the better. They have no knowledge that there is a path to a better life, let alone have any idea how to go about following that path.

"You can't make any money in radio unless you're a star, so I'm in the coffee business."

— DON ECKLES

A radio job in McCook, Neb.

Linda's Culbertson High School Class of 1974 senior photo.

It's so important for kids to finish high school. Once you've done that, all avenues are open to you. Community college, university, technical or trade school, work study programs, internships, mentorships, military or volunteer work programs, any or all of it. If you don't finish high school, the deck is stacked against you. Climbing to a better life is going to be very hard.

Understanding that kids have those challenges as they grow, I believe it's up to those of us who can help, to help. We need to find ways to get the message out to every kid, and even adults, that you CAN have the life you want. You have to work towards it, and you have to be willing to make some sacrifices along the way, but it's there for you. Find someone who can help you along the way.

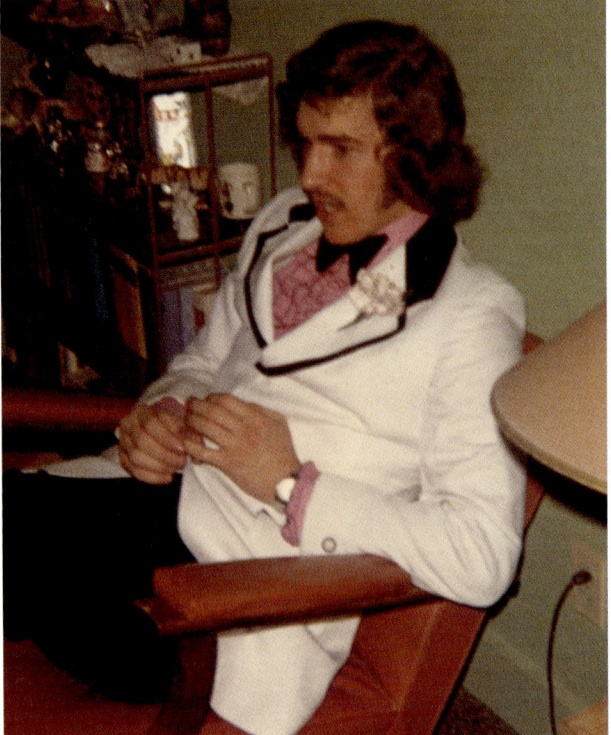

Don meets Linda at her home to go to the 1974 Senior Prom at Culbertson High.

After finishing Brown Institute, I got a job at KICX Radio in McCook, Nebraska, and met Linda Talley there. She was a cheerleader at Culbertson High School, and I was doing broadcast play-by-play for a basketball tournament in western Nebraska.

We dated and, after we married, we were living on next-to-starvation wages. I was making $100 a week as a radio announcer and Linda was making $50 a week folding sheets and towels at a laundry facility in McCook. She was just out of high school.

Dumb decisions — mistakes — can be great learning opportunities if we allow them to be. One of my first "dumb" decisions was that I started selling vacuum cleaners on the side in the evening to make extra money. I'd make a commission of $125 every time I sold a vacuum cleaner. I was good at it, partly because I have a gift of gab. One week I sold five vacuums. I was making more money selling vacuum cleaners part-time than I was making in radio full-time.

Linda Talley, head cheerleader for Culbertson High School, 1973-74.

"He was a radio announcer, and he was up on the stage. I was a cheerleader down on the floor right there. He smoked back then, so the other cheerleaders and I would go out on his break and ask him to play a song on the radio, or just talk to him.

"I was interested. That was on a Wednesday, and on Thursday I asked him to come to the concession stand and I'd give him some free popcorn. We just kind of got to know each other. And then he asked me out on Friday.

"Not long after, we were in the car parked by the school, and Don asked me if we could have a life together, or something like that. And we were kind of goofballs. We'd go up on the football field and run around and tackle each other."

Linda Eckles

Linda was homecoming queen as a senior and graduated in 1974.

The guy who owned the vacuum cleaner business offered me $150 a week guaranteed to do that. So I quit my radio job to sell vacuum cleaners — a bad decision.

It turned out that I wasn't as good at selling vacuum cleaners as I thought. These ladies were listening to me on the radio, so they were happy to let me in and talk about vacuum cleaners. Once I wasn't on the radio, that benefit went away. Not only that: I hated selling vacuum cleaners. I left a job I loved for one I hated, and if you hate your job, you're destined to fail.

Soon after that, we moved to Red Oak, Iowa, to be closer to my folks, who had moved to a farm near Griswold. I stayed with them for a few days when we came back. I took a job with Presto-X, the pest control company. •

"I had lived in Culbertson, in the same house, my whole life. Then we moved to Red Oak. I assumed we were going to be planted there the rest of our lives. I had no idea we were going to go on a lifelong adventure."

Linda Eckles

Linda's father, Harold Talley, co-owned the Firestone store in McCook, and her mother, Maxine, was secretary at the school. "I couldn't get away with anything," Linda said.

Don proposed and she accepted. On March 1, 1975, a year after their first date, they married.

Linda and Don working their very first garden at their home in McCook.

CHAPTER 2

GETTING JOBS
SIDE BUSINESSES TEST OUR METTLE

WE LIVED IN RED OAK, Iowa, while I worked for Presto-X. I was making $800 a month, which was twice what I was making in McCook. You have to remember that in 1975, $10,000 a year wasn't a great living, but it wasn't a bad living either. And it had insurance and benefits, and so Linda and my mom said, "Oh, yeah, this is the job for you." I quickly realized that I don't like rats and I'm afraid of snakes.

Ladies would call to say there were snakes in their basements and they wanted me to go down and find the snakes. I didn't want to find the snakes, for crying out loud. That job wasn't for me.

In those days many homes, including ours, didn't have laundry facilities so you took your clothes to the laundromat. In Red Oak, there was a laundromat right across the street from my house. When I would go in to do my laundry, I would visit with the owner of the laundromat. He was there to empty the quarters from the machines and clean the place. All I saw was him with bags of quarters every night.

I thought, "Wow, that guy is taking out bags of quarters. I need to be doing that." One day the guy told me he was selling the laundromat. I had no money, but he was willing to sell it to me on a contract, a seller-financed deal.

Now I'm going to be the one with bags of quarters every night.

I loved that whole idea of doing my own thing. I found out that there's more to it than just taking quarters out of the machine. Machines actually break down, and kids stuff things down the toilet and flood the floors. It became a real deal.

I was over there on my back fixing washing machines and dryers. I was my own boss, but I was also working for Presto-X.

LESSONS LEARNED

You leave school and you think you're really not very bright because everybody's just after you. There are a lot of kids that leave school and they think they don't have it. And what they don't have is an interest in school. But they have an interest in something. They're good at something.

Several years ago we developed this whole thought process called "Be Amazing." We believe that everybody has amazing in them. It's just some people, a lot of people, don't know it. Your amazing isn't going to be the same as everybody else's amazing.

That doesn't work out real well long-term because you can't serve two masters. Anytime I got an opportunity to work at the laundromat I was doing that, which meant the Presto-X stuff started sliding. The day came when Presto-X let me go. I was okay with that. Linda wasn't okay with that.

The laundromat didn't go broke. We just didn't make any money there. One night someone went in and started a fire. We had purchased some dry-cleaning machines that I thought would elevate the business, and we had 50-gallon drums of cleaning solvent in the back room. Those things were going off like bombs, and the building was destroyed. That was the end of the laundromat business.

"We each had jobs and then we had these side businesses. We had the laundromat and we had a golf cart and we put a freezer on the back. By that time my daughter had been born, so she'd sit on my lap and ring the bell. We'd go around town all day long, ringing the bell and selling ice cream, buying Bomb-Pops for 25 cents and selling them for 75 cents. We just went out and did it and hoped we made money. We didn't have any idea about the cost of goods or a budget.

"We did pretty well. At least we thought we did, back then."

Linda Eckles

Linda worked at Pizza Hut but also helped with the laundromat, cleaning machines and collecting the money. Their first daughter, Chandra, was born in Red Oak.

After the laundromat and the ice cream wagon, my third business was a cafe in Stanton, Iowa. One day while still working for Presto-X, I was spraying for pests at a real estate office, and the guy there asked, "You don't know anybody who wants to own a restaurant in Stanton, do you? Because the owner had a heart attack and he's selling the business for $25,000 including the building, and he'll sell it for $500 down and carry a contract."

Again, a seller-financed deal.

I was a young guy who didn't know anything about owning a restaurant, but it sounded pretty good to me. I didn't have much money, but I had $500. I bought the restaurant, which turned out to be a little better than a break-even proposition. I learned some valuable lessons there about people management.

The cook and the head waitress had been there forever, and I was 21 years old. At first I wasn't aware that they had wanted to buy that restaurant, but soon I found out. Word got back to me that they were talking about me behind my back. I decided to explain to them how life works, so I sat them down one day and said, "Look, I know you wanted to own this place, but I own it, and if you don't stop talking about me I'm going to fire both of you."

The lesson I learned here is that it's not a good idea to explain how life works to two 59-year-olds when you're 21 years old, especially in a town of 700 people, most of whom are either related or friends. I wasn't wise enough to visit with them and get to a point where we could all feel better about this whole deal. I made the situation very uncomfortable, and my business went south fast.

Soon after that, a guy I knew was visiting me. He said, "Boy, I've always wanted to have a business like this." And I said, "Good news. I'm going to make it happen for you." I sold him the restaurant for $40,000 just six months after I bought it for $25,000.

None of my businesses were doing what we needed to support the family, so I was also back in radio. I was at WOW Radio in Omaha, making $1,100 a month, which was a lot more than I made in McCook. It was 1977, so $14,000 a year wasn't terrible, but it wasn't great. Interestingly, Eric Fox was my boss there.

After the cafe sold, I ran into a guy who had an A&W Restaurant for sale in a neighboring town. He had operated that business successfully for 19 years, although it was a bit run-down. I've always been kind of an aggressive guy, so I took that extra $15,000 I had just received for the sale of the cafe, mortgaged pretty much everything I owned to borrow another $4,000 and signed another seller-financed deal.

> "When my dad passed away in 2020, I took my whole family to my school, and to my church where we got married and the house I lived in. It was really fun to show my grandkids where I grew up. They got a football and played on the same field where we met."
>
> — LINDA ECKLES

The owner showed me how to open and close the place and how to cook a hamburger. I went to A&W school for a week and learned how to make root beer. Now I was in the A&W business.

As a young guy, I figured I could clean the place up, add drive-up speakers and, because I was a hard worker and, I assumed, smarter than the previous owner, I could really make this into something special.

We had carhops who went to the cars to get the orders and then delivered the food. The speakers cut down on my need for as many carhops because now they were just taking food out to the cars.

Several lessons learned here. First, I not only wasn't smarter than the previous guy, I wasn't as smart as him. Second, while the speakers seemed like a good idea, they didn't do anything for sales but they set me back $5,000 which I didn't have. Third, I knew nothing about cost of goods sold, cost of labor as a percentage of sales, or really anything else about running a business effectively.

One day a guy from the Iowa Department of Revenue stopped in to ask me why I hadn't been paying my payroll taxes. "Payroll taxes?" I asked. There was more to running a business than handing food out the window.

We scratched out a living with the A&W for a couple years. Then McDonald's opened up down the street, which seemed like the end of the world then, but eventually turned out to be a really good thing.

We went broke pretty much immediately, going from $300 to $400 a day, which was fairly good at the time, to about $60 a day overnight. I was frying hamburgers in Linda's skillet because the stoves went down and I couldn't afford to get them fixed.

I lost all of our money, everything I had borrowed and everything I put into the A&W. I look back at it often and realize that if I hadn't gone broke in the A&W business, I wouldn't be in the coffee business. I'd still be there flipping hamburgers, scratching out a living. ●

POPULARITY

Ward Combs owned Presto-X, and one day he found out I went to Westside High School. "My daughter went to Westside, too," Ward said. I said, "Yeah, I know Debbie." What I really meant was I know who Debbie is. She has no idea who I am. She was a popular girl, and I was just a screwball.

So he calls her and says, "Hey, you're never going to believe who I'm sitting here with. Don Eckles." Long pause. "Don Eckles." Long pause.

I think he even said, "You want to talk to him?"

She must have said no, because he changed the subject.

— DON ECKLES

CHAPTER 3

RACING THE IDITAROD
CHALLENGES, SUCCESS IN ALASKA

THE FIRST FEW YEARS of our lives had been a bit chaotic. When my time with A&W ended, we moved to Alaska for four years. I worked as the overnight guy at KFQD-AM Radio in Anchorage and got $1,400 a month, which was $300 a month more than I was getting at WOW. Again, I was a young guy. I didn't realize that the cost of living in Alaska was a lot more than the cost of living in Omaha.

To get a better job, Linda was taking business classes at Anchorage Community College.

I was on my way to work in Anchorage one day in 1979, and traffic was stopped to let mushers cross the road as they headed out on the Iditarod dogsled race. I thought, "Man, that looks like the adventure of a lifetime. I need to do that."

Alaska is a different place. People have a different mentality. It's kind of refreshing, honestly. People are outdoors everywhere. The Chugach Mountains surround Anchorage on three sides. Cook Inlet is on the fourth side.

The value of this story isn't about the excitement of the adventure of a lifetime, a race from Anchorage to Nome. It's about what I learned about myself.

The primary lessons here were first, the lack of serious thought and reflection of my 24-year-old mind, and second, the fact that I'm not nearly as tough as I thought I was.

What was I thinking? I was a 24-year-old radio announcer with no experience living in the wilderness. The northern part of Alaska in the wintertime is brutally cold. There is danger everywhere. Yet I decided that day in 1979 that I wanted to participate in that race the following year.

Linda was pregnant with their second daughter, Traci, when the family, including older daughter Chandra, drove to Alaska for Don's new radio job. "I was sick the whole way," she said. "I remember Don's mom was so upset with us because we were taking her granddaughter away. Now I totally get that."

There was a lot to do. I contacted Joe Redington about the steps necessary to participate in the race. Joe is known as the Father of the Iditarod. I met Joe and Susan Butcher, who lived on Joe's property, to discuss steps: Lease a dog team, buy a sled, feed 14 hungry dogs for a year, practice every day for a year to build up strength in the dogs and myself, pay the entry fee, finish qualifying races and get the time off work. Nothing to it.

Looking back at the lack of consideration I showed for Linda and the girls at that time reminds me of how self-focused I was. I mean, think of the time commitment that I made without regard to how it impacted them. Think of the financial commitment.

There are a million stories during that year of preparation, but suffice it to say, I got through that year of training and headed out on my adventure on March 1, 1980, my five-year wedding anniversary.

The seasoned mushers had a strategy of running four hours, then feeding and resting the dogs and themselves for four hours, then heading out again. If I remember correctly, my starting position was No. 51 out of 62 mushers. I passed team after team with my strategy of running until I was tired, maybe 10 hours, then stopping and resting. The first night I was near the front of the pack when I stopped to sleep.

Teams of dogs and mushers race across 1,049 miles of Alaskan wilderness, from Anchorage to Nome, in the annual Iditarod dogsled race.
PICRYL.COM

I fed the dogs, laid my sleeping bag down on the ice, took off my cold and frozen gear and climbed into my sleeping bag to sleep. It wasn't many hours later that I discovered that laying my sleeping bag directly on the ice was not a very good idea. My body heat caused a bit of melting, resulting in a wet sleeping bag and a cold musher.

After a couple of days, I decided that I didn't need a camp stove and propane, which were extra weight for the dogs and me. If I had a chance to win this thing, I needed to simplify. I had seen several mushers cooking the old-fashioned way, with a fire they built from wood they gathered. I didn't realize that wood was scarce in certain parts of the journey. At times, I was feeding the dogs frozen meat, and I was eating frozen food myself.

There were times on the trail when I was lonely or afraid. When you're mushing along in the darkness alone, it's just you and the dogs, and the sound of a sled gliding across the snow. Very quiet. Very dark.

You realize how magnificent it all is and how much danger is all around you. There could be open water that you don't see until it's too late. There are moose, which hate dogs. There are wolves which kill and eat dogs and people. There are hazards which can cause serious injury or death. You begin to realize just how small and insignificant you are in the scheme of all that.

> "I actually thought I'd never see him again. He's just going out into the wilderness — 'See ya!' I made a map of his route for my girls, and each night when we'd hear on the TV where they were, we'd get a marker and mark it off so we'd sort of know where he was.
>
> "I made all these little dog booties for their paws and made food for him. It's frozen, but he could put it on the campfire and cook it. I kept thinking somebody will be there to help him if he needs something."

Linda Eckles

One of the requirements of the race is that all mushers have to take a mandatory 24-hour stop at one of the checkpoints. These checkpoints were welcomed because there were people there. You had someone to talk to for a short bit, and maybe a bite of decent food. At a few of the checkpoints, people would allow mushers to sleep in their homes, usually on the floor in your sleeping bag, but at least it was inside in the heat.

At my stop, a young teacher and her husband allowed two or three of us to sleep in their home. They fed us, played cards and checkers with us, laughed with us. When my 24 hours were up and I headed back out into the wilderness, I actually teared up.

I realized how lonely I was. I remember being surprised by the emotion I felt. I realized that I wasn't nearly as strong as I thought I was.

It wasn't that I wasn't strong, but maybe more that I learned that I really did need people in my life. I wasn't as able to just handle the world as I thought I was.

I missed Linda and the family. I was lonely. I didn't know what any of that meant then, but I know now how much we need each other. How interconnected we are. And that's a good thing.

The last day I was out, it just seemed like it was never going to end. It was 56 miles from Ruby to Galena, and I told myself, "When I get there, I'm done." I was on the Yukon River, and it was 40 below zero, and I went out on the river, which made it even colder because you're on the ice.

I didn't stop to feed the dogs, I didn't stop to eat, I didn't stop for anything. I expected to be there around 1 or 2 in the afternoon, maybe 3 o'clock. It got to be noon or 1 o'clock, and I'm going down the winding river, and every time I'd go round the bend I'd think I'm going to see Galena. Finally I saw a lady up on the bank, and I hollered at her, "How far to Galena?" She said, "Twenty-six miles." I was just barely past halfway to my stopping point, 300 or so miles short of the finish line.

Physically I was in great shape, but internal strength and wisdom are important, too.

At 24, I thought I could do anything. Because I actually thought I could win this thing, I did things differently from the dozens of seasoned mushers who had done this many times. I don't have to tell you how naive and foolish that was. I had no chance for anything other than the adventure of a lifetime. If I had wisdom then, I would have known that. Instead, I had exhausted myself and my team by the time we got to Galena. Still a great adventure, but not one I was able to complete.

After a couple of years in Anchorage, I got an offer to be program director at KVOK Radio on Kodiak Island, so we moved. We loved Kodiak, and we both did well there.

In the 1980 Iditarod, Don made it to Galena, nearly 700 miles, before stopping.

TRUE LOVE

The night we moved to Kodiak from Anchorage, everything we owned was in this Subaru hatchback. We were going to drive to the ship which was going to take us to Kodiak. Everything was loaded, and it was just raining cats and dogs, it was the middle of the night, and we had the bed frame in there. I went to close the hatch and the window of the hatch hit the bed frame and shattered. I had to get a big piece of plastic to cover the window, and Linda said, "Can't we just turn around? Can't we just not do this?"

No, we were out of the apartment. We had no place to live, it was raining. We had to go.

Poor Linda, being married to a guy like me has been a struggle. But she loved me, and she still does love me and that's the only way she's made it through this whole thing.

— DON ECKLES

Linda applied at several places for work and was hired at a dental office, doing well with patients and learning how to manage an office and even make dental X-rays. She was really good at it. Customer service is her thing. Her salary went from $7 an hour to $14, a good wage at the time.

"I liked that job. I really like people, and I felt bad for them when they came in. We had people come in from the bush who had never been to the dentist. I was at the dental office for three or four months when I was offered a job at the courthouse which paid almost double what I was making at the dental office.

"I went to my boss and told him what I was going to do. I wanted to be fair to him. And he said, 'If you stay I'll pay you double your salary.' So I happily stayed.

"He really needed the help, and he believed I was a good employee."

Linda Eckles

Don, with the mic, was promoted to operations manager of KVOK, "The Voice of Kodiak Island."

Within a short period of time, the owners of the radio station moved away and I became operations manager.

My base salary was $2,000 a month, up from $1,400 a month in Anchorage, plus I received 10 percent of advertising sales over the previous year. We were doing really well. Previous year sales were $30,000 a month and now we were doing $50,000, $60,000 or $70,000, so I was getting $5,000 or $6,000 a month. Forty years ago, that was a lot of money. We were stashing much of it away.

Man, the station sounded good, and the advertising was rolling in. My commission checks were larger than my salary, by a good bit.

Eventually, foolishness enters the picture again. As the money rolled in, it wasn't long before I realized that I'm really good at this. I should buy my own station and make this money for myself. In 1982 I bought a little radio station in Clarinda, Iowa.

Ah, the lessons just keep piling up. •

After years in Alaska, their daughters, especially Traci, were no longer familiar with their grandparents. "We just said, you know, we have to go home," Linda said. "We loved Alaska, but we have to go home and let the kids know their family."

LESSONS LEARNED

I learned one of my best life lessons in Alaska. I was running the radio station at 26 years of age. The other businesspeople were old enough to be my parents or even my grandparents. At Chamber events or Rotary dinners I would be the life of the party. One night on the way home from a party at one of their homes, Linda said, "Do you have to always be the funny guy?"

That hurt because it was true. And besides that, I didn't want to be the funny guy. I was just trying too hard to fit in. These people all had more experience. I was using humor to make up for what I perceived that I lacked. But I wanted people to take me seriously as a businessman, not as a comedian.

I decided that from that day forward I wasn't going to be "that guy" anymore. I'll always have a sense of humor, and I don't mind having fun with it, but I'm not going to be the entertainment. I was going to focus on being the kind of person that I wanted people to see in me.

CHAPTER 4

IOWA, AGAIN

MIDWEST JOBS AND LESSONS

I WAS 26 OR 27 years old and I was not a very deep thinker at that point. I didn't think about why I was doing so well in Kodiak. I figured, it had to be me. I'm a good sales guy, and I'm good on the radio and people are listening.

Turns out, I was pretty good at radio and ad sales, but not nearly as good as I thought. If you think about it a little bit, what's the difference between Kodiak, Alaska, and Clarinda, Iowa? In Kodiak, people could listen to us or the local PBS station, which was playing Mozart and Bach and doing a little news. That was it. Everybody was listening to us, and everybody was buying advertising.

In southwest Iowa, KQIS was not on an island. You could get radio stations in Omaha, Des Moines, Kansas City. There's a monster down the road called KMA in Shenandoah. There's a pretty good-sized station in Creston and other stations in Red Oak and Maryville, Missouri. People could listen to 100 different radio stations.

Then the farm crisis hit in 1982 and small-town businesses were crushed. Banks closed, implement dealers closed, furniture stores closed, clothing stores closed. Those were the advertisers. We basically spent the next four and a half years going through every dime we had or could borrow. We didn't take bankruptcy, but we lost every dime we put down on that radio station. We gave it back to the guy I bought it from, because we didn't have any money to go on any longer.

When the Clarinda station was running into trouble, I took a job at KFAB Radio in Omaha on the weekends — running my station during the week and doing news on KFAB on weekends, working for Kent Pavelka. That was kind of fun because they paid me really well and because Nebraska football — which KFAB broadcast — was only on TV three times a year, plus bowl games. Everybody was listening to KFAB, and I'm doing the news during the games.

LESSONS LEARNED

My mom was a tiny investor in KQIS in Clarinda. I called her and told her I was going to give the radio station back — I was out of money and there was no hope. She said, "Oh, my gosh. You worked so hard, don't do that. Let me lend you $10,000." So she did, and six months later we were out of that $10,000.

It doesn't help to borrow money if the fundamentals don't change, because unless something changes fundamentally, you're still going to run out of money.

As KQIS was failing, I bought a little route sales business called J.T.'s General Store, which used to be the Jewel Tea Company. They were around for nearly 100 years. You'd see those trucks going around, selling catalog items and groceries and things like that, and the drivers actually owned their business. It was like a franchise in that we used the company's name and products, but we didn't pay a royalty on sales. Instead, they made their money by up-charges on all of the products we sold and purchased through them.

That was a model that worked great back in the day, and it was a life-changer for me. Over the next several years I learned much about leadership but even more about financial planning, budgeting and other basics, which helped me move to a different place in my own personal, and future business, life. I slowly but surely started to accumulate some personal wealth. Not much at first, but over time, a significant amount.

I had a route in Omaha and I did really well with it. As it was a sales business, I found success quickly. After about six months, the company asked me to sell my route and go to work teaching other people how to run their routes. So I did that, and they transferred me to Kansas City as district manager. I found success there as well and moved up the ladder fairly quickly.

I was making good money, and after about two years they asked me to become a division manager and move to Dallas. We left Kansas City and put money down on a house in Arlington, Texas. We were still staying at the hotel in Dallas when I got a call from the home office in Chicago. It was a Friday evening call, saying, "You have to be in Chicago tomorrow morning at 8 o'clock for a meeting." And I remember thinking, "That's never good." •

Don and Linda with Chandra and Traci in Clarinda, Iowa, in 1983.

Left: Don with a J.T.'s General Store sales award.

CHAPTER 5

CALIFORNIA, HERE WE GO
DON GETS A PROMOTION TO THE LAND OF COFFEE

I ARRIVED IN CHICAGO and walked into a room with a bunch of people I didn't know. The bank had foreclosed on the company and another company had bought them. These people were basically introducing themselves and telling us they're going to make some changes. The guy who was taking over told me, "We don't know what we're doing yet, but we do know that you're still part of the plan."

They closed the office in Dallas and moved me to Sacramento, and I ran the state of California for them. The funny thing about that was when I was being promoted to division manager in Kansas City, I had told management that I would go anywhere except California and Buffalo, New York. But there we were in Sacramento.

I ran their California business, but their model was becoming outdated with increasing pressure from large department stores and more families becoming multi-income. I began to notice that people were disappearing from the company. It dawned on me that one day I would get tapped on the shoulder. I'm learning to think a little ahead, so I left that company.

Until then, I really didn't understand how any of these businesses actually worked. I was basically just going to work every day doing what I did best. Never did I step back and think about why customers might or might not want to come to my business. I didn't think about customer acquisition or retention. Now I believe that thinking and doing something about those things is likely the difference between getting it right, or failing.

> "Don was a division manager with J.T.'s General Store, and I got in that business, too. I bought a route and I went door to door with a van. It's like a Sears on wheels.
>
> "If a customer wasn't home, I put a note on the door that said, 'If you need anything, here's my number, and I'll see you next time.' I had product in the van, and I knew all the products because we used them. I could tell people what they were and how to use them. It was easy for me to sell those things.
>
> "I was one of only 10 women in the whole company who owned sales routes. I was in the top 10 of all sales routes, so I was excited about that."

Linda Eckles

A J.T.'s General Store class in April 1990. Linda is front row, right.

I left J.T.'s to buy another route sales business out in California that I ended up disliking. But I'm a guy who believes you're usually uncomfortable in a new job for a short time. It was a company selling electrical components. I owned the business but sold the company's products to railroads, the airlines and places like that.

I tell people, a new job is awkward. You don't know what you're doing, you don't know who you're doing it with, you don't even know where the paperclips are. You're just uncomfortable for a while, so never quit a job immediately. Wait awhile and see if you settle in. I think that time frame's a year. I disliked that job on Day 1 and I disliked it on Day 365, so on Day 366 I sold that business.

LESSONS LEARNED

I tell our employees all the time, if you like what you do and you make a living at it, and you like the people you do it with, you're 90 percent there. Stop jumping the fence for a few bucks. The grass is not greener on the other side of the fence, it just isn't. Life is not just about money.

GETTING FIRED

At a different company, I disputed their recruiting methods. The business promised its sales people would make $35,000 a year, and I hired people who gave up good jobs based on the promise. But it turned out they didn't make that much, and I discovered that company leadership knew most sales folks weren't making that kind of money.

I told my boss, "I could hire guys and tell them they're going to make $25,000. Let's be honest with them."

I got a nasty letter telling me, "You hire people and I'll run the company." Days later, the boss came out and I was fired.

We had already planned to move back to Nebraska and start a coffee business after our daughter finished high school. I was making so much money doing that on the side that I started thinking about not doing Scooter's Coffee. But they fired me, so that made it real easy to come back and start Scooter's.

— DON ECKLES

CHAPTER 6

JAVA? WHAT'S THAT?
SWEET BUSINESS BLOSSOMS IN FOLSOM

Sweet Things & Java

Linda Eckles

"We went to Nebraska and brought back the Whirla-Whip machine. We were at church, and a friend knew we wanted to start a business. She said, 'You need to have specialty coffee in your business.' We hadn't heard of specialty coffee. She took Don uptown and showed him what this specialty coffee business was all about."

WE HAD DECIDED to start a Whirla-Whip business, selling ice cream. We added coffee as kind of a last-minute aside. We opened a store in Folsom, California, called Sweet Things & Java.

We went to a specialty coffee store and I had a cup of the coffee. I was shocked. Up until that point, like everybody, I drank Folger's or Maxwell House or whatever coffee. I didn't know there was such a thing as specialty grade coffee. I'd heard of arabica coffee beans, but specialty grade coffee is like the best of the arabica coffee beans.

As jobs disappear, some start own firms

By Paul Schnitt
Bee Staff Writer

Linda and Don Eckles chucked the rapidly shrinking corporate world to open Sweet Things and Java in Folsom.

'The company had been downsizing for years. It became apparent to me that it was just a matter of time before I was going to be the one who would be tapped on the shoulders.'
— Don Eckles

Don Eckles left a well-paying job and good benefits as a regional sales manager for a wholesale distributor and opened a business with his wife, Linda.

About a year ago, the Eckles opened a snack shop in Folsom called Sweet Things and Java. They now employ five high school students part-time.

"People said, 'Man, you're crazy to invest all this money when times are tough and people are going broke,'" Eckles said. "Well, we're not going broke."

Unique offerings at Sweet Things and Java

Whirla whip machine, delivery and catering have top billing

By Muriel Brounstein
Telegraph-News Correspondent

A Whirla whip machine is what makes Sweet Things and Java different from other ice cream and yogurt shops, according to owners Don and Linda Eckles.

The couple said there are only four Whirla whip machines in the state; the nearest is in the Bay area.

The machine is capable of making thousands of flavors by using vanilla or chocolate yogurt or ice cream as a base and adding fresh fruit, cookies, candy or nuts.

The difference between Whirla whip and other yogurt or ice cream is that the ingredient is blended throughout the portion, not just served on top.

"This is a real mom and pop shop and I'm the pop," said Don, in his traditional introduction.

"We've been thinking about having an ice cream and coffee shop for ten years. It's a family dream come true."

In July last year, the family began their venture. Daughters Chandra, 17, and Traci, 14, also work at the shop.

Don runs the shop, which is open from 6 a.m. until 9 p.m. Monday through Saturday. He is in by 5 a.m. so he can begin muffins and rolls which are freshly baked on the premises every day.

The caramel corn, made from an old family recipe, is also made daily.

For those on a diet, there are very low-fat muffins featuring only one gram of fat, as opposed to the usual 10 to 15 grams.

Also, there are non-fat and low-fat yogurts, cafe mochas, cafe lattes and capuchinos.

Sweet Things and Java also features a shaved ice machine, which makes a soft snowcone, created with a Whirla whip machine. The shop also offers a delivery service and fresh baked muffins and rolls.

homemade pies and gourmet teas and sodas.

There are outdoor tables with umbrellas and the inside is decorated like an outdoor ice cream parlor with awnings and lattice work.

The pink, green and white decorations invite the customer to sit down, relax and take a break.

Linda runs the delivery service which is somewhat unique. She is becoming known as the lady in the navy blue van with the burgundy apron and a big smile.

There are existing routes in Folsom and Orangevale where her customers expect her at certain times.

Her delivery hours are 8:30 a.m. to 5 p.m. on Monday through Friday and 9 a.m. to 2 p.m. on Saturday.

She brings baskets of muffins, rolls, fruit, freshly ground coffee beans, caramel corn and chips on her route. Also in her van is hot coffee, mochas, sandwiches, salads, homemade pies and cold sodas.

Yogurt and ice cream are available on request.

Customers can call in for special orders or to have an office meeting or lunch catered, with no minimum number requirement.

"It's a very personalized service," said Linda.

"If I don't have an item with me, I'll go back to the shop and get it," she added.

The Eckles are also community-minded. They belong to the Orangevale Chamber of Commerce. Don coaches his daughter Traci's American Softball Association team and they have supported the Folsom Frontier Little League.

Sweet Things and Java is located in the American River Plaza (Albertson's), 9500 Greenback Lane, suite 32. For information, call 987-7933.

Don and Linda put Chandra and Traci to work.

I was like, "Holy cow, this is really different and better." So that's where I first discovered it. We opened Sweet Things & Java, a store with delivery service.

Linda would pull into a car dealership or a repair shop and go in, and they loved it. She'd bring their afternoon snack, or they'd call in and order some ice cream in the afternoon, no delivery charge. It was all right around in that area, but we worked really hard and scratched out a living.

"We added coffee, and we had popcorn and the ice cream machine. We made our own popcorn using Grandma's recipe for caramel corn and made little bags that said 'Grandma's Best' on them. Don went in early and would be in the back making cinnamon rolls and muffins.

"I had a basket full of muffins, cookies, cinnamon rolls and other products. In the back of my van I would have airpots of coffee and hot chocolate.

"I had a route, going business to business. It got to the point where we were doing more business through my route sales than what was actually just coming into the store.

"Back then we had these telephones that you put in your car. People started calling in orders for me, and it got hectic because Don would call me and say, 'You need to get back here because you have 15 drinks you need to deliver.' The route was a big part of our success."

Linda Eckles

Linda's basket of muffins, cookies and other snacks boosted sales for Sweet Things & Java, but delivering to customers took time and effort.

When we sold Sweet Things & Java, we put coffee carts in two California legislative buildings using the name Always Espresso. I worked at one and Linda the other, going to work early and finishing about 2 p.m. I also had a job helping a large coffee company develop an office coffee business in California. So we were very busy.

"At that point, it was frustrating. We had four businesses in three years, and we both were working other jobs, too. And that's why I said, 'Can't we just get jobs like normal people?' It wasn't fun all the time.

"I went along for the ride. I love him, and I just knew in his heart that he wasn't able to be an employee."

Linda Eckles

Java is shorthand for arabica coffee beans originally grown in Java, Indonesia, which produce a full-bodied coffee with low to medium acidity.

Java Detour in Sacramento caught Don's attention in the mid-1990s.

Linda Eckles

"Don's mom and my dad were our biggest fans. My dad and Don's dad loved that our coffee shops in California were actually working. They thought it was pretty cool.

"When we told them we were moving back to Nebraska to start a coffee shop, they were upset with us. They thought nobody would want to pay $3 for a cup of coffee in Omaha because no one understood or even knew there was such a thing as specialty coffee.

"Both of them had had surgeries and we were clear out there in California and we couldn't be with them. I said to Don, 'We just have to move home.'"

One day I'm driving along out in north Sacramento and I saw a guy building a little shed, actually hammering and putting up the building himself. I stopped and visited with him and he said he was building a drive-thru coffee place. I went back and told Linda, "This guy's on to something."

It was called Java Detour, and when he opened up I'd go in the morning and sit and watch the cars go in and out of there. That's where I got the idea for Scooter's Coffee. We were working like crazy delivering coffee and running a store, and his customers were coming to him and driving in and out quickly. •

LOSING MONEY

Linda has been willing to do whatever we've needed to do, a great willing partner. Imagine being married to a guy like me who's gone broke so many times, and I've got one hare-brained scheme after another — all with good intentions. I've always tried to be a good guy, but that doesn't mean I don't make mistakes or dumb decisions. I've lost all our money or I've lost our investors' money more than once. That's hard, and she has always been there.

— DON ECKLES

CHAPTER 7

COMING HOME
STARTING ANEW IN OMAHA

OUR OLDEST DAUGHTER was in college, and when our youngest daughter graduated from high school in 1997, we came back to Omaha even though we didn't have a location yet for our first store.

Linda and Don, ready for orders at Scooter's Java Express.

It took a long time to find our first location in Omaha. From the landlord's standpoint, the bank's standpoint, somebody comes into your office 30 years ago, and says, "I want to build a little kiosk in your parking lot and sell $3 cups of coffee." It's like, "Get out of here. What are you talking about?" We started looking a couple years before we moved back from California.

We had saved up $50,000 or $60,000. We had sold our coffee business out in California, but we hadn't sold our house yet. We knew banks weren't going to lend us the money to build the first one, so we didn't want to use that money to live on. We got jobs here, but we didn't want to be unfair to the employers because we were going to quit as soon as we found a place to build a coffee store.

I got really lucky because Herman's Nut House was advertising for a delivery driver for the holidays, which was just perfect. It was a minimum wage job, but it's paying the bills and I don't have to live on my savings and I'm not being unfair to an employer. Linda got a job waiting tables at Grandmother's Restaurant, doing the very same thing. It was great, and we were able to be honest with them and tell them we were going to go into the coffee business. We did that for about six months, and it worked out really well.

The very first Scooter's Coffee location was known as "Scooter's Java Express."

I finally found a place on 24th and Cornhusker. It wasn't ideal, but we remodeled that building. It was an old Chinese restaurant and had been Carole's Pasta-to-Go, owned by Carole and Gary Thrasher. We leased that space for $1,000 a month. Gary and I laugh about it now because I believe that he was sure I'd never make it. He probably thought he would get a few months' rent while he figured out what to do with his building. But 20 years later we were still only paying about $1,300 month, because it had a 1.5 percent rent escalator every year. The rent was practically nothing. Later we bought the land and tore down the building and built a new one.

Linda was in the window all the time at that store. I was the guy making the drinks. •

SCOOTER'S COFFEE IS BORN: OUR FIRST STORE OPENS IN BELLEVUE, NE

THE ARTIST BEHIND THE ORIGINAL LOGO

Stacy Peterson was good friends with Chandra Eckles at a California middle school and later worked at the Eckles' early coffee carts in downtown Sacramento. Don and Linda knew she was a budding artist and asked her to create a logo for the first Scooter's Coffee location in Omaha.

"They were really excited about the drive-thru idea, which was kind of a new concept in Omaha," said Stacy, now Stacy Spaeth, an interior designer in Sebastopol, California. "They wanted something that was mobile and quick, drive-thru and get coffee.

"I came up with a little guy driving a coffee cup car with drips splashing. He's kind of excited, smiling and driving real fast, like he's hopped up on caffeine. They thought it was cute and liked it."

When the first Scooter's Coffee store opened in Omaha, the Eckles bought Stacy a plane ticket to visit Chandra in Omaha and add graphics to the building, including a scene on the drive-thru exterior depicting the coffee car guy.

Today's Scooter's Coffee staff fondly remember the speedy coffee guy from the first logo. He appears on some T-shirts and other memorabilia and hustled back as a prop for the company's 25th birthday advertising campaign.

The logo has evolved over the years, eventually becoming the current red circle around the company name.

"We're happy with our logo now," Don Eckles said. "It's hard to read words when you're driving or far away, but this is something you can recognize from a distance."

Traci and Chandra in a cutout replica of the first logo's coffee cart during a photo shoot for the 25th birthday campaign.

WHY THE NAME?

I called Traci "Scooter" only because she played high school and college softball and she was not fast. She was a great hitter, great defensive player, but not fast, so I called her Scooter to annoy her.

One day when we were trying to think of a name for the business she said, "Why don't you call it Scooter's?"

I thought, scoot in, scoot out, okay, I like that. So that's what "Scooter's" is for. So actually I did call Traci "Scooter," but the company is not named after her.

Our goal was to keep customers happy by providing fast service that allowed them to "scoot in and scoot out" with their orders.

— DON ECKLES

CRANE COMPETITION

When we came to town, Crane Coffee was already here, although we didn't know it. When I called down to the Health Department for permits for a coffee drive-thru place, the guy there said, "Oh, yeah, Crane Coffee is doing the same thing at 129th and Maple."

That was the first I'd ever heard of them. And it's like, "What the heck is that?" And I drove out there, and they're building a drive-thru coffee kiosk, and I thought, "You've got to be kidding me." Someone had beaten me to it.

They also had taken over the old Goodrich Dairy store on Cass Street. Steve Hammerstrom was very aggressive, too. He and his wife, Paulette, were building stores all over the place in the 2000s.

Some of their stores, I would say, "Why is he building a store there? It just doesn't make sense. Maybe I'm doing something wrong, because he's got more stores than I do."

OMAHA WORLD-HERALD ARCHIVES

Turned out I was right. Steve and Paulette were new at this, too. We were both doing deals we shouldn't have done, getting some right, some wrong. They built eight stores and never went beyond that.

One day we heard that Crane was building a store right down the street from our first store, a drive-thru window at the Fantasy gas station down by Bellevue West High School. It just made me sick, and Linda was so worried. What are we going to do?

I had started to figure out that we were getting to know our customers well.

When they came in, Linda knew their names. I said to her, "Why would anybody leave you to go to Crane? Our coffee's better and you're in the window. They don't have that." And that turned out to be the case.

LESSONS LEARNED

Think about what you do and do it well, and you have a high probability of success.

But we didn't know that for sure, and the night before they opened at the Fantasy I came home from our second store, at 72nd and Farnam. My son-in-law was at the dinner table and he said, "I bet you're sick about the Crane thing, aren't you?"

"What Crane thing?" I said.

Crane had put yard signs up and down Cornhusker Road, including right in front of our store, saying they were opening the next morning. And they had them on the exit ramp off Highway 75. I joked with people that I was so upset that I went over in my pickup and accidentally ran over all of those signs.

As it turned out, the Fantasy store wasn't a great location. They only lasted six or eight months down there, and then they were gone.

After several years of being competitors, Steve died. I wrote Paulette a letter saying, "I know we've been competitors, but I've been an admirer of you guys for a long time. If you need any help with leases or other things, just call me." I got a nice note from her saying she appreciated the thought, and we got together for coffee after that.

Paulette eventually sold the business to a couple who changed the model. They actually started selling dinners and alcohol. One day I saw a billboard that said, "Prime rib dinners, 2 for 1 at Crane," and I thought, "Uh, oh, the beginning of the end." I called that owner and said, "If you guys ever want to sell the business, we'd be interested in buying." She was in our office the next morning.

We decided to buy the business, but we realized that might be kind of a conflict of interest with our franchisees. So we talked to two of our investors, Keith and Linda Graeve, the parents of Todd Graeve, now our CEO. They agreed to buy Crane Coffee with the stipulation that they buy coffee from us. They kept the Crane name for six or eight years. Eventually we bought Crane from them and just converted them all to Scooter's Coffee stores.

Best of Omaha, 2004:

COFFEE SHOP

1. Scooters Java Express
"The coffee market in Omaha has changed dramatically in the past three or four years," Don Eckles says. "A few years ago, people could be successful in the specialty coffee business without a lot of effort. Now, consumers are very aware of quality and taste." They're also aware of who is No. 1 in Omaha — Scooters. Want more? Visit www.scootersjavaexpress.com

SCOOTERS JAVA EXPRESS

2. Starbuck's
3. Crane Coffee

30 www.omahapublications.com • January/February 2004

CHAPTER 8

COFFEE TO GO
THE EARLY DAYS OF SCOOTER'S JAVA EXPRESS

HAVING AN IDEA for a coffee shop is only the first step, even though we were experienced in the retail business of specialty coffee. Once our store opened, we had a lot to learn, and obviously we were the only two employees. On the first day, we were in there ready to open at 5:30 in the morning and nobody's coming and nobody's coming and nobody's coming, and the lights are on. It's like 6:30 and we still hadn't had our first customer.

We were in the back room talking when all of a sudden the speaker beeped and Linda said, "Oh, my gosh, what do I say?" All of this preparation we had done, we hadn't thought about what we were going to say when the speaker beeps for the very first time.

Linda's original smiley face name tag and, facing page, early smiley face stickers for the top of each cup.

Linda Eckles

"I think I said, 'Welcome to Scooter's. What can I get started for you?'"

Chuck Williams, one of the first customers, charmed Don and Linda with his Texas accent.

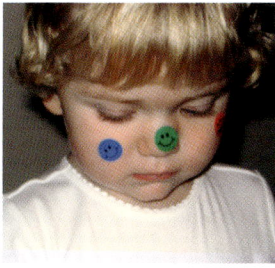

Bailey Kipper with stickers.

WHY THE SMILEY STICKERS?

In 1998, Linda Eckles bought happy face stickers and placed them on every drink she sold. It was her way to say, "Have an amazing day!" Customers loved the added touch so much they often commented on how it made their day a little more special.

One of the first customers was Chuck Williams, who is still a customer to this day. Chuck would pull in and the beeper would beep, and he'd say, "What tiiiiime is it?!" in his Texas accent. We'd say, "Oh, Chuck, time for a great cup of coffee. Pull on around."

We had a lot of customers who didn't know about specialty coffee back then. They would order a cappuccino and then they'd come back around and be upset because they thought we cheated them. They were getting a real cappuccino, but they were used to getting a bigger drink from a machine in a gas station that said it was cappuccino. It was this hot, milky water with powder and a little coffee flavor and some vanilla stuff. It tasted good, but it wasn't a cappuccino.

So we'd say, "I think you want a vanilla latte." We'd work with them. I was trying to get them to understand what a great cup of coffee really is.

That first store was a great experience. Sales were slow and we got to know the customers so well. Linda had been giving out stickers at our places in California, and it was her idea to put a happy-face sticker on each coffee cup.

Linda Eckles

"We had our first store. And then when Don said, 'Hmm, I think we can have seven, or maybe even ten,' and I thought, 'No way.'

"Then we opened the second store. He had his and I had mine. I would go to the grocery store and get the milk and the whipped cream and just take it to the stores. I'd do all the laundry for both stores."

By then Starbucks was becoming a monster in the coffee business. They didn't do drive-thru, but other places were starting to. We had to figure out what we were going to do that's different.

This is a loyalty business. People love their coffee place because you drink coffee every day. So what are you going to do that gets a customer out of somebody else's line and into our line?

With Linda at the first location, Don operated the second at 72nd and Farnam Streets, which later moved two blocks to 72nd and Dodge Streets, Omaha's busiest intersection.

We knew Starbucks was coming to town one of these days. So we had to ask ourselves, "Why would anybody choose us? What are we going to do to separate ourselves to compete with those guys?"

What we decided is this: We're going to focus on great drinks, higher quality than almost anybody, really fast, and a big smile. Some of our competitors have pretty good coffee, but we needed to be better. Most of our competitors use cheaper syrups and powders and cups where you have to use a sleeve. We use real syrups and high-quality sauces, and the cups are double-insulated so you don't need a sleeve and it keeps the coffee hotter.

And then the drive-thru has to be fast, and we work on the relationships. When you see somebody every day, you get to know their voice. And everybody has the headsets on, and you recognize somebody's voice. That's the triple latte lady, triple mocha guy, whatever.

LESSONS LEARNED

This is a loyalty business, a relationship business, and customer service builds relationships and loyalty. Some fast-food places have pretty good burgers or ice cream or other things, but their customer service is pretty mediocre. There's more to business than just handing out whatever we sell. It's not always true that people do business with people they like, but that's really foundational to success.

Don and Linda, in the Scooter's Java Express store. Above: The first menu.

BE NICE

I was at a drive-thru food place and I had asked for a "pup cup" because our pup was in the car. And when she handed us our food and she started to close the window, I said, "Is our pup cup there?" And she just looked at me and then she closed the window and went and got the pup cup and came back and opened the window and handed me the pup cup and closed the window. She didn't say, "Thanks" or "Oops, I forgot" or "See you next time," just closed the window again.

Businesses should realize that if you're nice to people, it's hard for them to not come back.

— DON ECKLES

A corgi enjoys a pup cup, a free treat with a Milk-Bone and whipped cream.

Always a smile from Linda as she fills coffee orders at Scooter's Java Express.

Back when we started, nobody was doing drive-thru coffee in a big way. We looked at that as our competitive advantage. We've continued to focus on getting faster and faster and faster, always keep the quality high. That's our model, and we'll kind of live or die with it.

We actually trademarked the phrase "Amazing people serving amazing drinks amazingly fast." We didn't use that as a marketing slogan, but we used it internally to remind people, that's what we do here. If we don't remember anything else, remember to make a great drink, smile at people and get them in and out really fast.

If it was just about the quality of the coffee, everybody would buy coffee from us because our coffee really is better. It's that relationship with the customer that's the difference, along with the speed through the line.

The relationship is important because customers do coffee every day. You don't do hamburgers or pizza or ice cream or fried chicken every day. You start developing an idea of who's in the window at your coffee store and you notice how you are treated. If we get to know our customers and they get to know us and they matter to us, we're never going to lose them. They like us, they like our drinks and we're fast. Why would you go anyplace else?

In his book "Good to Great: Why Some Companies Make the Leap ... and Others Don't," Jim Collins says you have to know what matters in your business and focus on that like a laser beam. Don't get distracted or take your eye off those things. Know why customers choose you, and then become great at those things.

We started this thing. We had the idea and we've worked really hard. But we've done nothing without somebody standing shoulder to shoulder with us all the way. •

An early loyalty punch card.

Scooter's Java Express opens a kiosk at Westroads Mall in 2000.

TRACKING GROWTH

Don and Linda opened Scooter's Java Express on March 23, 1998. A week later she began logging sales by time of day to identify busy hours.

Linda holds one of the original log books, which were simple spiral bound notebooks with carefully recorded hourly sales and expenses.

She pasted letter-stickers on the front of a 100-page pocket notebook, spelling out "Scooter's Java Express." A new notebook followed each year.

"We wanted to keep track of our growth," Linda said. "We wanted to succeed and we wanted to make money. It was just fun to see what we were doing."

First-day sales totaled $93, well below Don's calculated break-even point of $340 and 108 customers a day. Coffee was $1.25, and latte $2. On April 4, Linda logged that she had bought batteries from a Chevron station for $2.76 cash. A week later, $2.08 for tape.

On Tuesday, Sept. 11, 2001, sales totaled $582.70. There was an extra note, circled: "Bombing."

The entry for Dec. 20, 2001, was surrounded by dozens of happy-face and candy-cane stamps: sales topped $1,000 for the first time. In black magic marker at the top of the page, Linda wrote "B.D.E.E." — Best Day Ever Ever.

"It took us a while to reach $1,000 in one day," Linda said. "And now it's just kind of unbelievable what the stores do in a few hours in the morning, much more than that." Don said there are good reasons to keep careful records.

"Back in the A&W days, I'd stick the money in my pocket and I'd stop and have a beer or a hamburger on the way home, and I'd pay for it out of the store's money," he said. "You're just flush with cash and you're just spending money — if you need it, you buy it, and whatever's left you put in the bank.

"Then all of a sudden the bills start rolling in, and it's like 'Holy cow! What just happened?'" •

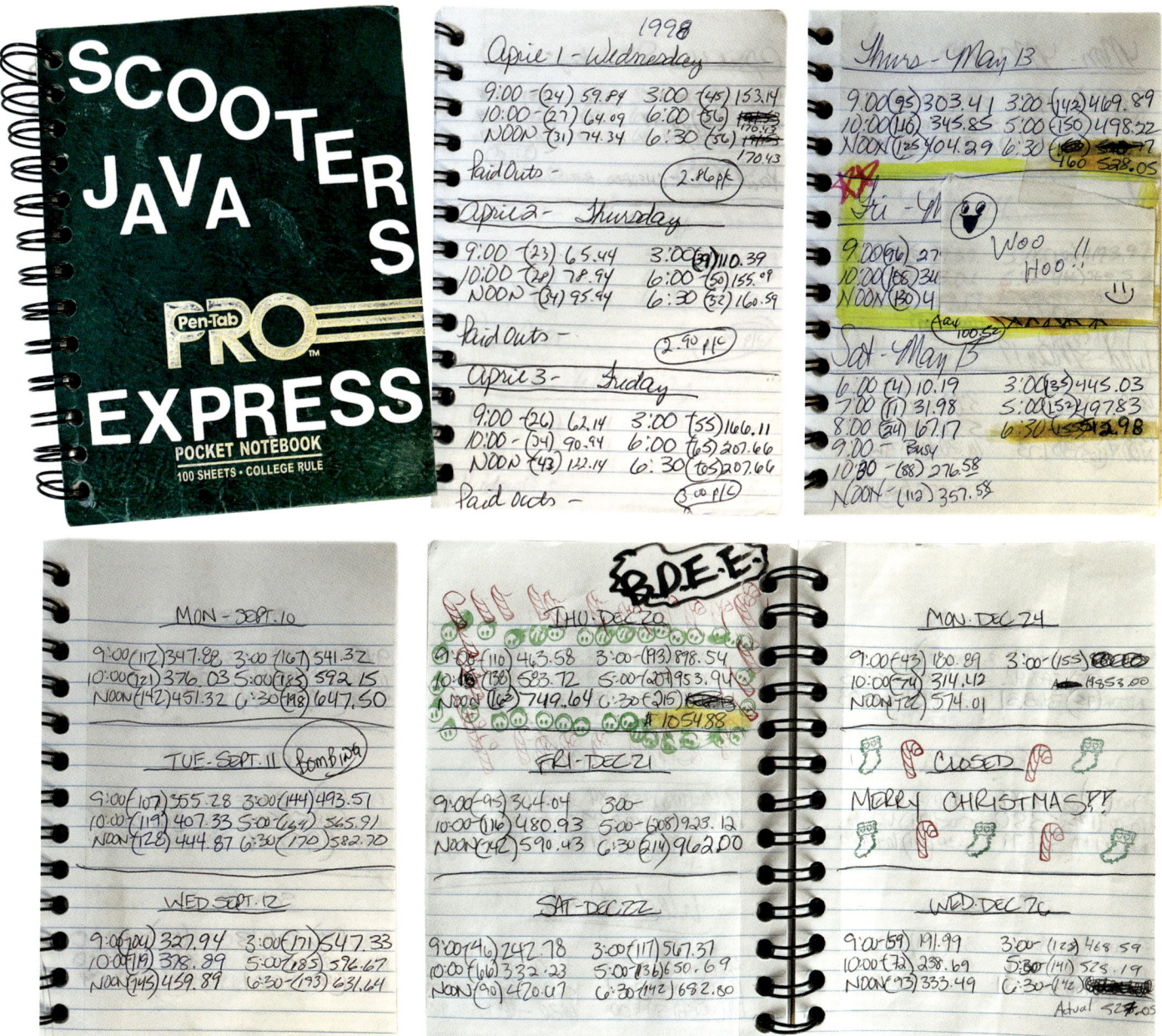

Linda's log books began April 1, 1998, a week after the first store opened. Sales of $651.09 on May 14, 1999, earned a red star and a "Woo Hoo!!" flap. Bottom row, a circled note on Sept. 11, 2001, reads, "Bombing." Sales passed $1,000 for the first time on Dec. 20, 2001, earning dozens of happy-face and candy-cane stamps and the label "B.D.E.E." — Best Day Ever Ever.

SCOOTER'S JAVA EXPRESS LOCATIONS

Scooter's Java Express took charge of delivering supplies to stores by expanding into a fleet of delivery trucks.

31st & Broadway, Council Bluffs, Iowa

156th & Pacific

132nd & West Center Road

138th & S in Millard Plaza

"You can't really think of a great restaurant that has great food and great customer service that ever goes broke. They just don't."

— DON ECKLES

A kiosk at Regency. Top: 120th & Blondo

SOLD, BOUGHT

Don Eckles once sold Scooter's Coffee.

It happened in the early 2000s when a group of friends, including Don, formed a company called SJE Holdings (named after Scooter's Java Express) and bought the coffee store business, leaving Don with some store locations.

"It was a mistake doing that deal," Don said. SJE changed the Scooter's Coffee model, emphasizing upscale coffee houses. "It didn't work."

Three years later, Don and another group of partners bought the business back, forming a holding company called Boundless Enterprises and restoring the focus to small, drive-thru stores.

Today, Boundless Enterprises is the holding company for Scooter's Coffee, Harvest Roasting and Boundless Real Estate Holdings, which owns real estate and company-owned stores.

LOGO PROGRESSION

2001

By 2001, we had five stores and people were already clamoring for more. We decided to start franchising the business in 2001. The first Scooter's Coffee franchise location laid the foundation for the hundreds of stores to follow. We updated our logo to reflect our continuing commitment to world-class coffee.

2003

Our name evolved to "Scooter's Coffeehouse" to reflect a more sophisticated image and attract coffee enthusiasts who appreciate a high-quality cup of coffee. The logo redesign and coffeehouse name brought a new era of the brand to life and helped fuel our reputation as a purveyor of premium coffeehouse products.

2011

The brand name was shortened to become simply "Scooter's Coffee," which is more inclusive of the drive-thru concept at our locations. We redesigned our logo with the new name and a streamlined graphic that reflects our commitment to quality coffee.

TODAY

Loyal customers continue to want more and more and so we keep growing, but we'll always remain true to our original Brand Promise: Amazing People, Amazing Drinks… Amazingly Fast!"® It's the cornerstone of our business, and the commitment we make to every customer, franchisee and employee of Scooter's Coffee.

The Caramelicious® is our signature drink! If you're new to Scooter's Coffee, you can't go wrong with ordering this rich, velvety, caramel gem.

CHAPTER 9

GROWTH BY FRANCHISING
FINDING PEOPLE WHO CARE

AFTER THE FIRST FOUR or five stores opened in Omaha, by 2001, friends and family members would come by and say, "Hey, I want to own one of those." I'd say, "Well, you can't, but thanks for stopping by." Even customers were asking about franchises.

Eventually we realized that maybe franchising isn't a bad idea. If you're going to have 10 stores or 20 stores, it's hard to hire people who care as much as you do. Franchising would be a great way for us to bring in people who care about the business as much as we do because they're buying a business and they'll take it as seriously as we do.

The first franchisees were friends and family, in Omaha only. Among the first outside Omaha were Tracy and Shawn Bouwens, who bought franchise rights to the Kansas City area. Also in the group was Tracy's brother, Todd Graeve, who would eventually join us as our Chief Financial Officer, then become CEO.

FRANCHISING EST. 2001

Brenda Rynders became the first Scooter's Coffee franchise owner when she opened her store at 36th Street and Highway 370 in Bellevue, Nebraska. The store is still open today.

"The Scooter's Coffee corporate support team cares deeply about our success in this business. They are constantly working to find ways to drive new customers to our stores while protecting the bottom line and profitability of our business."

— TRACY BOUWENS, MULTI-UNIT OWNER, NEBRASKA, KANSAS & MISSOURI

"Scooter's Coffee was starting to pioneer outside of Omaha just a little bit, mainly Lincoln and Kansas City. I think there were only 25 or 35 stores in the system. And my sister and I and my brother-in-law bought a 50-store deal in Kansas City.

"Probably not the wisest on our part, frankly, to do so many stores. A leap of faith. Part of that is that when you meet Don Eckles, there's an inspiration there. He casts hope. He believes with all of his heart, with absolute conviction that we can make it.

"And frankly, back then there weren't easy days. Stores weren't doing what they're doing today in terms of volume. They were doing a fraction of that. They cost less to build, but you had to kind of fight and scrap a little bit. And so my business partners and I went on a journey. When are we going to find financial oxygen in Kansas City? Through some grit, we stuck it out and found our way.

"Don would drive down to Kansas City and look at sites with us and teach us what he felt we needed to have in a site and validate that for us. We built a trusting franchisor-franchisee relationship at that time."

Todd Graeve

Franchising has grown rapidly in recent years. In 2021 Scooter's Coffee signed 200 deals with franchisees representing about 800 stores, and more in 2022.

Our franchisees look at a lot of franchise concepts, and hundreds apply for ours. We have "Be Amazing Day" every month for prospective franchise holders and ask them, "What brought you to Scooter's Coffee?" Over and over, they say it's the company's core values and the culture that attracted them.

It's also about that relationship with the customer. If all you want to do is hand a cup of coffee out the window and hopefully take a wheelbarrow full of money to the bank at the end of the week, you might as well just buy a hamburger franchise or a pizza franchise and hand a sack of hamburgers out the window, because that's not how our model works. It's important that we don't lose focus of that.

Prospective franchisees attending an online Be Amazing Day receive a virtual tour of the top-performing Scooter's Coffee store, located in Council Bluffs, Iowa, from franchisee Chandra Kipper, left, and her store director, Brooke Jensen. "Everybody needs a Brooke, but you can't have mine," Chandra said.

Scooter's Coffee executives, from left: Joe Thornton, president; Don Eckles, chairman; and Todd Graeve, CEO, at Owner Immersion for new franchisees.

Owner Immersion is a conference in Omaha for new franchise holders who have signed their agreements and paid their fees and have had some training and are working to open their first stores.

At those sessions I tell them: "We already have your money. We don't need to be here. We're paying to rent this room and feed you while you're here. We're here because what we're about to tell you matters. We have two or three days to pound into your brain how easy this model works and how well it works. If you do it right, if you get the right real estate, if you get the right people, if you train them well, it's hard to mess it up. If you don't get these things right, you might do okay anyway, but you won't kill it. So, when we say 'no' to you on a real estate location, that's because we don't want you to lose all your money."

> "Is this a good fit for you, a good fit for us, before we step into this together?"
>
> — TODD GRAEVE, CEO, DURING BE AMAZING DAY WITH PROSPECTIVE FRANCHISEES

GOBS OF MONEY

At an Owner Immersion meeting, a franchise holder raised a question about problems finding a site. I said, "Let's talk about it." The franchisee said, "Right now?" I said, "Yeah, let's talk about it."

They were shocked, because having trouble with real estate is kind of like dirty laundry. But it's good to talk about that. We want the franchisees to know. There's no such thing as a perfect site. There's a lot of great sites, and you can make gobs of money on that site or not do it because you're waiting for the perfect site that's never going to be available.

— DON ECKLES

At Owner Immersion, franchisees have an opportunity to learn how their business works, how important it is to get the right real estate deal and to hire people who really like people. All of that matters, because if you get this business right, we just crush it. We still have people in our system who insist on not getting it right. They want to do a cheap real estate deal. They think they can live in Omaha and run their store somewhere else, or they want to keep their jobs in a different city and see how it goes before moving there. That's not how it works. We turn people down if we get a whiff of that. You're done right then.

If you don't believe the model's going to work and you want to keep an ace in the hole, that's fine, but I can tell you that our model always works if we get the fundamentals right. But it's not going to work if you're in Omaha and your store is somewhere else.

It comes back to integrity. It's easy to take people's money. They'll write us a check for a franchise fee. We don't want that. We want people to get the magic of our business, to understand who we are and who want to be a part of that and say, "I get it. I love what you guys are doing. I'm going to do it. You tell me what to do and I'll do it."

Location is everything. Bill Kipper, Don, Dustin Kipper and Eric Gabriel at the groundbreaking for Scooter's Java Express at 120th & Blondo in West Omaha.

We want people who understand who we are as a company. We want to be the kind of company that we are today, five years from now, 10 years from now, 20 years from now. That matters to us.

I'll take the third best person who believes in our core values and can do the job over the best person who doesn't. That applies as we go looking for real estate and as we're expanding to new markets and doing other things.

We're still an underdog in a lot of places. When we got to Cincinnati, for example, there wasn't a strong local player, so it was mainly Starbucks and Dunkin'. Nobody had ever heard of Scooter's Coffee, so we are still the scrappy little guy there. We pay the same rent as everybody and we'll do the volume that anybody else will do, but they've never heard of us so we still have to be aggressive and scrappy.

But I like that attitude anyway. We don't want things to get too easy. We want to remember that everybody wants the best sites. We don't want to make deals just because we can. We want to make sure that every deal is going to work out well for our franchisees. I tell our franchisees that we make money whether you make money or not. You sell a dollar's worth of coffee and we get 6 cents. But if you only sell a dollar's worth of coffee, you're going broke and so are we, shortly thereafter.

Omaha World-Herald, March 11, 2004:

72nd, Dodge: joe to go, go, go, go, go

By STACIE HAMEL
WORLD-HERALD STAFF WRITER

Don't look for velvet Elvis paintings anymore in the Fuddruckers restaurant parking lot at 72nd and Dodge Streets.

No longer will you find vendors there hawking paintings, rugs or beanbag chairs. You will, however, soon be able to drive up for a cup of coffee. Or four or five.

A four-window Scooters Java Express drive-through is under construction and is expected to open May 1, said Don Eckles, company president.

In addition, Starbucks Coffee Co. will open a drive-through and sit-down shop next-door in a strip mall under construction. It is expected to open this summer.

Eckles said his drive-through will be unique.

"We're excited about it because it will provide access for four cars at a time. I don't know of any other coffee stores around like it," he said.

Starbucks will be one of the retail tenants in a 12,000-square-foot strip mall under construction on a two-acre tract just south of the Scooters site. The land was purchased in February by former Nebraskan Don Bourn for $2.2 million in a deal that also included the nearby former Wherehouse Music Store at 7010 Dodge St. Bourn is president of Bourn Properties of Tucson.

Bridget Barrett, Starbucks regional marketing manager, said the new shop will offer a choice.

"We're excited to offer the opportunity to come into the cafe and sit down and relax, or if you're in a hurry, you can go through the drive-through."

Eckles said he also is confident his product can compete with the coffee next door.

"We're not going to go away just because they came to town. We think we have a better cup of coffee," he said.

Eckles has eyed the 72nd and Dodge corner

See *Java:* Page 2

Java: Coffee to go coming soon at 72nd, Dodge

Continued from Page 1
for several years, he said.

"That's obviously a fabulous corner.... As far as access and visibility and all those things, an argument could be made it's the best corner in town," he said.

The Scooters drive-through will be a franchise, operated by four of the five partners who own the Fuddruckers franchise, land and building.

More changes are planned for the corner, said Rick Windrum, one of the partners, along with Travis Freeman, Steve Schell and Mike Kucera.

Plans for Fuddruckers include a new menu in April, interior remodeling, and a new facade and awnings outside. The parking lot will be expanded to the south — where Douglas Street was abandoned — to make up for spaces lost to the coffee business.

"This whole corner will look like a totally different corner a year from now," he said.

Just one vendor still will sell merchandise at the corner, Windrum said: holiday lighting by Brite Ideas Decorating, founded by Fuddruckers partner Freeman.

Eckles said the 72nd and Dodge Scooters is one of four now under construction, which will bring the chain's total to 16. Others are being built at 168th Street and West Dodge Road, to open by late May; 180th and Q Streets, mid-April; and 175th Street and West Center Road, late June.

From 1998 to 2001, Scooters operated a location at 72nd and Farnam Streets, just two blocks south of the new site. That restaurant now is called New York Chicken and Coffee Lover's Express. Scooters Inc. paid a fee to be released from a noncompete agreement with the current owner, Eckles said.

The national Starbucks chain and locally owned Mid-America Coffee Specialties, which operates Crane Coffee shops, are the metro area's next largest chains with seven locations each, not including counters inside groceries or discount stores.

"It's a competitive business, I'll tell you that," Eckles said.

Scooters comes out ahead in being local because its beans are roasted in town, he said. And there are other advantages, too.

"I grew up in Omaha ... I think a lot of people would just as soon deal with the local guy," Eckles said. "We feel like we are able to stand up and compete."

"It's hard to find the right site. Everybody wants the right site, not just us. McDonald's does, Starbucks does, everybody does. We're all competing for the same site."

— DON ECKLES

Omaha World-Herald, April 17, 2006:

Recognition

- The Greater Omaha Chamber of Commerce will recognize the following businesses at their Omaha 25 Excellence in Business Awards luncheon of May 16:
- "Emerging Business of the Year Award" to Scooter's Coffeehouse Inc.
- "Minority Business of the Year Award" to Midwest Maintenance Co. Inc.
- "Not-For-Profit Organization of the Year Award" to Boys and Girls Clubs of Omaha.
- "Small Business Advisor of the Year Award" to Rod Jewell, Foundations Financial Group-Mass Mutual.
- "Small Business of the Year Award" to Dingman's Collision Center.

Excellence in Business Awards to:
- One to 15 employees: Egermier Wealth Management Group; Midwest Impressions Inc.; Performance Group Inc.; Signs By Tomorrow; and The Training and Consulting Connection.
- 16 to 50 employees: Adult and Pediatric Urology Nox-Crete Inc.; P&L Capital Corp.; RK Digital; and Thrasher Basement Systems Inc.
- 51 to 100 employees: Brown's Medical Imaging; CSSS.NET; Home Instead Senior Care; Regent Financial Group Inc.; and Sergeant's Pet Care Products Inc.
- More than 100 employees: 21st Century Systems Inc.; FirstComp Insurance Co.; Focus Solutions; NetShops; and Titan Medical Group.

Don and Linda held their first franchise meeting at a Holiday Inn in Omaha in 2002.

Todd Graeve

"Don and Linda built their stores, they began franchising, and it was hard," Todd said. "Franchising takes dedication, and there's a deep responsibility to people that are trusting us, many times with their life savings. And so we take it very seriously from the days when Don first started franchising to today.

"It costs a million dollars to build a Scooter's Coffee store, and so we want to really make sure it works for them. And it is working. The model's really strong financially.

"We take it very seriously, and that's a part of the legacy of Don and Linda. They'll lay awake at night thinking about a franchisee who might be struggling.

"As the company has grown, the DNA of the franchisee has changed a little bit. We don't really want to bring in the 200-store, multi-concept franchisee who wants to add to their portfolio. That's really not who we are.

"We want to help small business people build an enterprise, a legacy for them and their family, maybe even generational wealth for their families. I think it'll always be that.

"How do we help franchisees build their own enterprise? What's their succession or exit strategy? How do you step out of the business and maybe pass along the reins of leadership to your son or daughter or to another leader? They can't do it on their own forever. Like Don and I had to, they need to begin to think about succession and surrounding themselves with talented folks to take their business to the next level or into the next season.

"How do we support that different DNA-type of franchisee who wants to go to 100 stores after starting off with three stores years ago? It's fascinating."

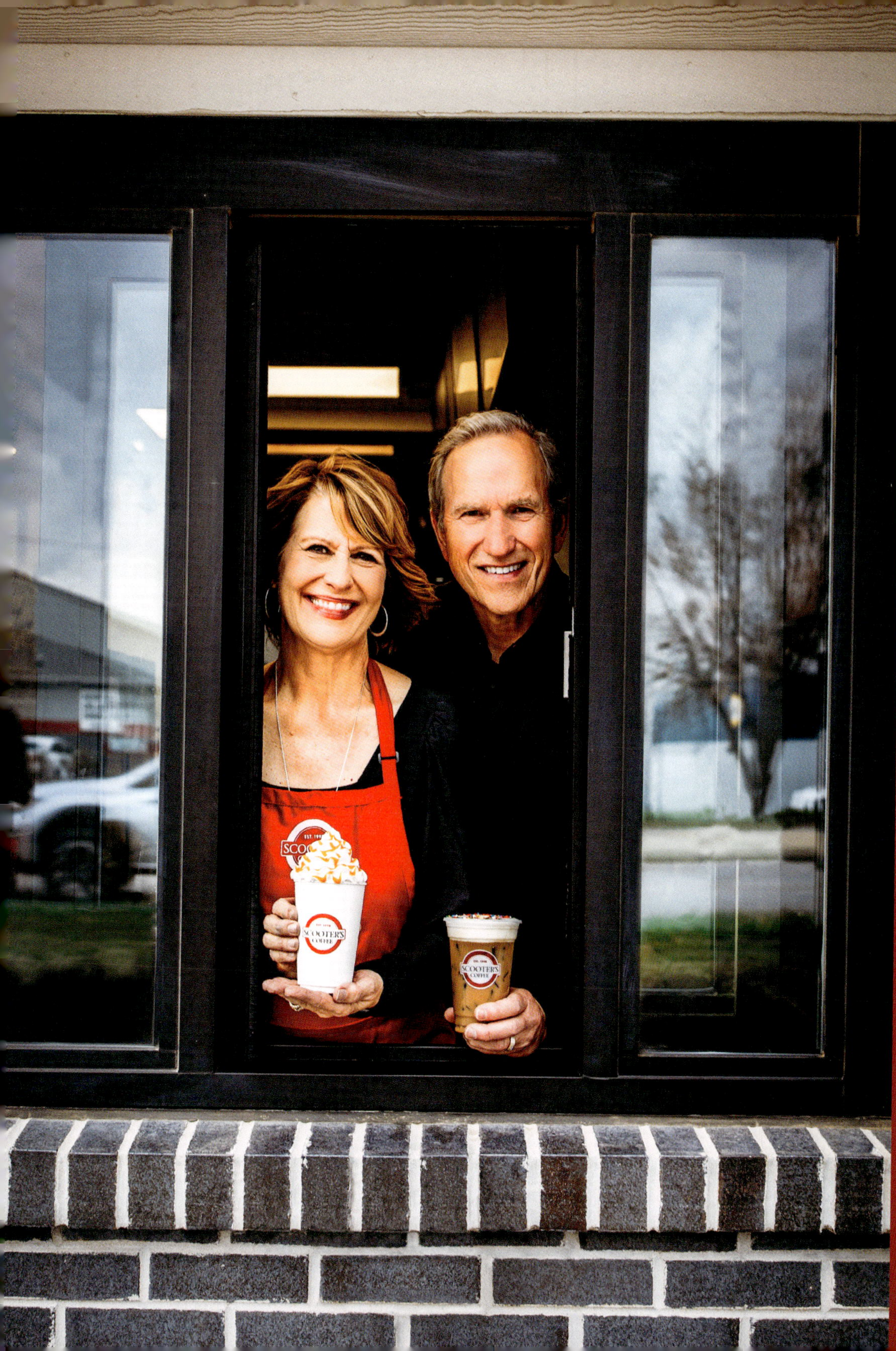

"We set a record of 206 cars in an hour at this store. We call that 'smiles per hour.'"

— FRANCHISEE CHANDRA KIPPER, ABOUT HER COUNCIL BLUFFS STORE, TO PROSPECTIVE FRANCHISEES DURING BE AMAZING DAY

NO PLACE LIKE THE GOOD LIFE

Imagine talking with people from Seattle, Dallas, Atlanta or Fort Lauderdale about moving to Omaha. Some of them don't get it. Yes, we have a couple weeks during the winter when it's pretty ugly, and two or three weeks in the summer where it's pretty hot and humid.

But other than that, this is a pretty darn good place. The folks are nice here. The opportunities are strong here. This is a great place to be. We can't recruit people by assuming that they want to be here. If you don't want to live here, I'm fine with that.

In 2002 Don and Linda, wearing hats in the back row, took the entire staff to Lake Panorama for a fun day in Iowa: from left, Bill Kipper, Chandra and Traci Eckles, Liz Mulhern, Melissa Mallow, Emmalyn and Jeannine.

But for us, senior executives must live in Omaha. The reason: If everything is remote, you never really become part of the "family." If that's the case, it's just a job. And if it's just a job, the day will come when another job comes along, and you're gone. We want people to become part of something special. People who want to help us do big things. People who are willing to roll up their sleeves and join us in building something that few are able to build.

I didn't coin the phrase "Nebraska, the Good Life," but I've always believed that it's true. I think we Nebraskans sometimes have an inferiority complex, allowing ourselves to believe that other places are better than here, that there's more to see and more to do at other places. Other places have mountains and oceans and huge amusement parks.

But Nebraska in general, and Omaha in particular, is a wonderful place to live and work. The quality of life here is spectacular — wonderful and friendly people, maybe an unmatched work ethic, great education system, an always strong economy. Incredible and varied restaurants. One of the best zoos in the world. An amazing symphony orchestra and theater community. Very strong local music scene. The College World Series, the Old Market, the Gene Leahy Mall and the RiverFront development project, and those are just a few.

We have a quality of life here that is unique and special. We need to not only know who we are. We also need to embrace that and tout it. We need to encourage our kids and our grandkids to see the world if you want to, but when you're ready to build your life, remember, there is no place like Nebraska. •

"We look for someone who's competitive, a team player, who can hold a conversation. Attitude, be positive, upbeat, energetic, no drama, motivated, excited to be here, happy to see people. The rest of it, we can train."

— BROOKE JENSEN, STORE MANAGER, DURING BE AMAZING DAY FOR PROSPECTIVE FRANCHISEES

GROW CONFERENCE

Annual Grow franchise meetings have grown along with the company. Grow 2023 will host hundreds of franchise owners and their families in Omaha. Don plans to hold future meetings in Scooter's Coffee's hometown.

Chandra, Linda, Don and Traci at the 2022 Grow Conference in Dallas.

"We're creating an infrastructure that can support growth. You rely on systems a lot more, and you have to really create relationships and trust people to execute."

—JASON METCALF

FRANCHISEES: JASON & RITA METCALF

Jason Metcalf was in Italy with his wife, pro volleyball player, Nebraska All-American and Olympian Nancy Metcalf, when his mother called: How about going into the coffee business with me?

Rita Metcalf had found Scooter's Coffee in an Omaha mall, liked the coffee and thought, "I've always wanted to be in the coffee business."

Jason had been accepted at a chiropractic school, but he changed direction and signed on with Rita, especially because Scooter's Coffee's values — Integrity, LOVE, Humility, and Courage — fit with his family. "We liked that Scooter's Coffee was local, based out of Omaha."

That was 18 years ago. Today mother and son are headed toward 40 locations in Lincoln and Oklahoma City.

"We love what we do and we enjoy working together," Jason said. "We have differences of opinion, but our values are the same and our goals are the same."

The Metcalfs are answering Scooter's Coffee's call for growth by existing franchise holders adding new locations, a strategy that Jason said requires expansive thinking.

"When you're operating one or two stores, you work the store, you do the orders, you can do what you need to do to fill the gaps and solve problems," he said. "As you grow, you need leaders who are experienced, high-integrity, emotionally intelligent people.

"We made eight leadership hires this past year and it's been life-changing, our best year yet, because of the talent we were able to attract. The biggest thing is our leaders' ability to bridge the gap between ideas and execution."

Businesses have to make money, Jason said, but sometimes leaders have to step back from short-term profits to set up the company for long-term growth.

"You have to focus ahead and staff to support where you want to be, because you can never get behind," he said. "When people get in trouble is when they're trying to catch up." •

FRANCHISEES: JULIAN & BRITTANY YOUNG

Julian Young was an entrepreneur before he knew the word. Growing up in North Omaha, Julian saw his first drug deal at age 8, was labeled a troublemaker in school and started his own business at 15.

"By 17 I was growing a very lucrative, profitable business using every single skill set that an entrepreneur would use to run a successful business," he said. "But I was running an illegal one."

Family problems, poverty, school troubles, and anger made him "disengage" from school and landed him in jail several times, even though he was not involved in gangs. "I was interested in money," he said. "We were poor and we wanted nice things. It intrigued me to see a sale happen and how quickly the money piled up."

By 19, he was standing before an Omaha judge, facing a 15-year prison sentence for several felonies. Then something clicked, partly because he decided he wanted to find out what God intended for his life.

"It became clear to me that I had hurt a lot of people and made a lot of bad decisions and that the first thing I needed to do was take responsibility," Julian said. "I told the judge, 'If you give me one more chance, you will never see me in your courtroom again.'"

The judge pondered for what seemed like an eternity and then agreed not to revoke Julian's probation. "I'm going to give you one more chance," he said, "but I'm telling you, if you even so much as sneeze in the wrong direction, you're going to prison."

Back in college — Julian had been kicked out twice before — a business professor at Wayne State College in Nebraska told him, "You're an entrepreneur."

"I said, 'A what?' I had never heard the word," Julian said. All through school, his different way of thinking had led him to believe he didn't have what it takes to be successful.

The professor had him join a group called Students In Free Enterprise, now known as Enactus. He succeeded in the group, met successful business executives and was inspired to start a consulting business to encourage new businesses to improve North Omaha, the traditional center of Omaha's black population.

He formed a consulting business, Julian Young Business Advisors, and a nonprofit, the Julian and Brittany Young Foundation, to spread entrepreneurship.

> "Selling drugs in college rather than on the street was a risk assessment. Lower risk, better environment, less competition."
>
> — JULIAN YOUNG

Brittany and Julian Young operate a nonprofit and a consulting business next door to their Scooter's Coffee location and encourage community members to use its meeting areas.

THINKING THROUGH

I hope we can help people understand the right way to do things, more along the lines of the thought process, about thinking things through and the way you treat other people and the way you should act in life.

— DON ECKLES

Former Nebraska football coach Tom Osborne became a mentor for the nonprofit group, but Julian needed more help on the business side.

He was a Scooter's Coffee customer. "Everyone was so nice. The service was good, the food was good, the coffee was good. I decided I had to meet the guy behind the business. I needed a business mentor."

He learned that co-founder Don Eckles was from Omaha, called the headquarters and left a long voice mail on Don's extension. Within a day or two Eckles called ("I was shocked. He had taken the time to listen!") and invited Julian to come to his office at 8:30 a.m. on Christmas Eve day.

Don gives a Scooter's Coffee donation check to former Nebraska coach Tom Osborne for his TeamMates mentoring program. Both men were mentors for Julian Young.

The Youngs and the Eckles cut the ribbon at Julian's store in Omaha's black community.

"It was kind of a small sense of validation, maybe a sign that I was onto something," Julian said. They talked all morning, the start of a relationship that lasts to this day and expanded to include mentoring by Linda Eckles of Julian and his wife, Brittany.

"Now the store I visited made sense, because Don's one of the nicest people you'll meet in your life," Julian said. "That's why customer service is so big in his shops. It's the passion of the couple that created this."

After several years, Julian and Brittany became franchise holders of the Scooter's Coffee location at 30th Street and Ames Avenue, a prominent North Omaha corner. Julian's grandparents had been savings and loan customers in the same building. It's a $500,000 investment by Scooter's Coffee.

Julian's vision is for the space to grow beyond a coffee house into a community center with meeting rooms and other facilities sorely needed by the city's black community.

The 30th & Ames franchise location opened in March 2018.

"There are so many other gifted entrepreneurial minds that are falling through the cracks of public education, a lack of exposure to opportunities," he said. "I felt like I could make a difference by engaging entrepreneurs in my community."

Julian and Brittany may or may not open another Scooter's Coffee location in Omaha, but Julian said other cities have neighborhoods that could use similar stores. "I would definitely help Scooter's Coffee open more stores in communities of color." ●

A BETTER WAY

I have a heart for kids. Kids in lower-income neighborhoods, for example, who maybe don't have mom or dad at home, or maybe don't have either one of them at home. They might be in foster care. They might be home but their folks just don't have any money.

Life is tough for them, and they don't have any idea it doesn't have to stay that way. It doesn't have to be like this forever. There's opportunity for anybody. But some of these kids just don't know it. They don't know that there are scholarships or grants or mentorships or work-study programs.

There are ways for everybody to rise above it, but a lot of kids don't have somebody to put their arm around them and say, "Hey, there's a better way, just stick with it."

— DON ECKLES

CHARITABLE ACTIVITIES

I tell the fable originated by the late Loren Eiseley, a Nebraska anthropologist and author, about a big storm that washed thousands of starfish onto a beach, where they would surely die. A young girl was picking up starfish and throwing them into the water when a man approached her and said, "Little girl, why are you doing this? Look at this beach! You can't save all these starfish. You can't begin to make a difference."

The girl bent down, picked up another starfish, tossed it into the water and said, "Well, I made a difference for that one."

That's the way we think about it. We want to help people. You can't solve everybody's problems, but for some people we can make a difference. And let's do things that can involve our customers.

THE PINK AGENDA

Breast cancer matters to people. Everybody's got a mom or a grandmother or a sister or a cousin who's died from it or they know of someone who is struggling with breast cancer. Our customers are primarily female, and we want to do things that help organizations that matter to our customers.

Scooter's Coffee stores sell Courage Cookies — sugar cookies with cream cheese frosting and pink sprinkles — and donate 20 percent of the sales to The Pink Agenda, a nationwide nonprofit that raises money for breast cancer research and support.

Scooter's Coffee customers bought enough Courage Cookies to donate more than $203,000 in 2022.

SCHOLARSHIPS

We sponsor scholarships to camps for children who wouldn't otherwise be able to go. Our Grit Scholarships are awarded to college students who have overcome problems and show their determination to succeed.

You don't have to go to a four-year university. You can go to a trade school or a community college. If you want to get on the ball and you've shown that you've had to persevere through some hard times, then apply for the Grit Scholarships.

WOUNDED WARRIORS FAMILY SUPPORT

We're a patriotic company. I've been to a lot of places, really good places, and there isn't a better country on Earth to solve whatever issues we have. It's important for us to remember that.

So I'm a big fan of first responders and people that dedicate their lives to protecting us and then, by the way, they're killed or they lose a limb or they have some struggles.

Wounded Warriors Family Support helps them in their efforts — mobility vehicles if they need to get around, or job training that fits whatever their disability is, or support for their families if they're killed, or many other efforts. •

Scooter's Coffee executives Bill Black, left, and Joe Thornton present a check to Wounded Warriors Family Support founder Col. John Folsom, with the cap, and Kate McCauley, CEO and president of Wounded Warriors Family Support.

CHAPTER 10

HARVEST ROASTING
OWNING OUR OWN SUPPLY CHAIN PAYS OFF

WHEN WE STARTED Scooter's Coffee, we were buying coffee from Java City in Sacramento. They had really good coffee, specialty beans for their seven stores, but they'd wholesale the coffee to us.

It wasn't ground, it was roasted. We'd get it through UPS in five-pound bags and grind it all fresh in the store, and you'd get it fresh, maybe a week old. Coffee, if it's roasted and packaged properly, is good for six or eight weeks for sure.

If you get coffee within a couple weeks of it being roasted, it's a pretty darn good coffee. And then you grind it there, 15 pounds of espresso, 15 pounds of Scooter's Coffee blend, whatever you need. The first store wasn't using a lot of coffee at the start, maybe $170 worth at the end of the week, maybe 70 cups of coffee a day.

But the problem is, if the UPS guy doesn't show up or something else unexpected happens, you're out of coffee. Then what? We learned from that how much it mattered to customers. The delivery wouldn't show up, so we'd go to the grocery store to buy some coffee beans. If you look at coffee in grocery stores, a lot of it is dated out a year. You can't do that, so we started buying coffee locally from a guy up in Sioux City, Iowa.

Don with the roaster at the second store.

LESSONS LEARNED

When the economy was tanking in 2008 and 2009, we were doing just fine, but we can't go out and borrow money to get through this thing. We've got to make sure we're living within our means.

We thought that all large roasters were roasting quality coffee, but this was a completely different product.

When we opened our second store at 72nd and Farnam in Omaha, I realized we needed to start roasting our own coffee. I went to Idaho, where they have a coffee roasting school and sold roasters. I brought one back and we started roasting our own in the store. We were going through about 100 pounds of beans a week. Roasting our own coffee wasn't easy — in fact, it was a lot of work. But we were able to control the quality and have fresh coffee, to flavor it or do whatever we wanted ourselves. That was kind of a cool deal.

Don's mother, Myrna, and Linda package coffee beans.

Now we import our own beans. We know farmers in the coffee growing regions of the world. We call it "relationship coffee." We know who is growing our coffee, and they know who is buying their coffee. Pretty cool. We have somebody that imports the coffee for us. We buy millions of pounds of coffee per year.

That was the start of Harvest Roasting, a sister company to Scooter's Coffee. Back 30 years ago there were very few specialty coffee stores around. We had to buy cups and lids from this guy, coffee from that guy, syrups and sauces from another guy. You're not getting good pricing at all because you're not buying much from anybody, and they don't really care about you as a customer.

So we picked up distribution rights to Monin, a French-founded syrup and flavoring company, and we picked up the rights to sell our own cups and sauces, all under Harvest Roasting. Now Harvest Roasting sells pretty much everything to our franchisees except milk. We use our own trucks to deliver nearly 99 percent of the products our stores need.

Josh Goad operates the roaster at the Omaha production and distribution center. Scooter's Coffee blends beans from around the world.

WE ONLY ROAST FROM THE TOP 10% OF COFFEE BEANS IN THE WORLD.

That's a big deal, but the bigger deal is we can control the cost for our franchisees. That's important because there are only a few costs that you can really control. Cost of goods matters, and Harvest Roasting allows us to control the cost of goods at the store level.

Cost of goods sold, labor, loan interest, utilities, royalties, credit card fees can get to 100 percent of revenue pretty quickly. We want to keep the cost of goods in a reasonable range. If coffee bean prices go up, or sugar goes up, or paper goes down, we can keep the overall cost of goods in the proper range.

Except when there's crazy inflation, we're pretty solid on those costs. Even with recent high inflation, costs to franchisees increased as a last resort, and a retail price increase compensated for that.

Owning the supply chain allows us to make sure we keep those costs under control. We can take a profit hit at Harvest Roasting and we can swallow losses for a long time, knowing prices will eventually come down and we will get back to making a little bit of profit on everything. Generally that works out well because some things will go up and other things will go down.

When the pandemic hit, other coffee stores ran out of products and had to cut their hours, which hurt revenue, and some are still closing in the afternoon. Owning our supply chain helped franchisees keep their stores open. We briefly ran out of Clorox wipes because of high demand one time, but nothing else.

Some suppliers add surcharges when inflation hits. We don't do that. It allows our franchisees to be whole in good times and bad. Our franchisees do well. They love their businesses and make a good living.

Nobody else in our industry has their own supply chain, owning the whole thing. That's a big deal. ●

Packaging coffee for retail sales, front to back: Ba Hatoo, Joe Meyers and Chris Baldwin.

NICK JARECKE

When a 2021 ice storm froze large parts of Texas, Scooter's Coffee stores there couldn't get milk, and drinking water was in short supply. Nick Jarecke's Harvest Roasting team sent special truckloads of milk and water to the stricken area.

"Owning our own fleet of trucks, we were able to deliver the same day from Omaha to those franchisees," Nick said. "It was the team saying, 'What's the need and how do we meet it?' We have strong connections with our franchisees and the communities they're serving."

Harvest Roasting came through in that emergency, but its true value is the regular day-to-day delivery of coffee, baked goods, cups and other supplies to the coffee stores.

"We buy all the ingredients that the stores need besides milk, and we ship it to them in our own trucks," Nick said. "It's what you call vertically integrated."

Nick has lived most of his life in Nebraska and has worked in Omaha for 16 years, joining Scooter's Coffee in 2019 after stints with food companies including Tyson Foods, General Mills and Kellogg.

"This is a unique opportunity to grow a hometown brand into a national brand and get more connected to the farmers and the supply chain," Nick said.

> "We didn't even know he was doing that — he just did it. People were becoming Scooter's Coffee customers who'd never heard of us before. We like being that kind of company, empowering people to do the right thing."
>
> — DON ECKLES, ON NICK JARECKE'S TEAM'S ACT OF GOOD WILL DURING THE 2021 TEXAS ICE STORM

Harvest Roasting trucks deliver supplies to Scooter's Coffee stores nationwide.

"The franchisees are our only customer. Having a clear view of that helps us make sure we give them what they need. We make it easy for them to grow with us and help them with their profitability."

— NICK JARECKE,
SENIOR VICE PRESIDENT

Top: Yu Lee, Paw Mu and Wah Wah run cake bites through a glazing process. Right: Wah Wah weighs cinnamon rolls. The bakery can produce and ship 30,000 cinnamon rolls a day.

Harvest Roasting has 200 employees, 50 trucks and six warehouses in Omaha, Kansas City, Atlanta and Dallas and plans to expand to 10 or more. "We're looking for a national and international footprint, coverage with our own equipment."

Harvest Roasting's bakery continues to tweak the store menu. "Some of our products, like our sugar cookies, are the best out there, in my opinion," Nick said.

During the pandemic, Harvest Roasting delivered everything the franchisees needed to stay open.

Drive-thru business was strong while many sit-down restaurants closed. Restaurant suppliers saw demand drop sharply.

"We provided some business for the suppliers, even if we had to order more than we intended so they would survive until things went back to 'normal,'" Nick said. "We love supporting our franchisees and helping them achieve their entrepreneurial dreams." •

Austin Sweazy stacks boxes for shipping from the warehouse in Omaha to Scooter's Coffee franchise stores.

Members of the Calderon Castillo family from Los Angeles visit the Don Cayito Farms in Costa Rica.

COSTA RICA

Love is one of Scooter's Coffee's core values, and it's important to Costa Rica coffee exporter and coffee grower Francisco Mena, too.

"If the producer doesn't give love, nurture and care to the coffee plant, we don't have a quality crop," said Mena, managing director of Exclusive Coffees in San Rafael de Alajuela. "The producer and the customer are the key elements in the whole supply chain, the ones that make this cycle happen."

That's why Scooter's Coffee and its sister company, Harvest Roasting, have a sourcing agreement with Exclusive Coffees, in turn directly benefiting hundreds if not thousands of Costa Rican coffee growers who plant, nurture, pick, process and ship millions of pounds of coffee beans annually to the Omaha-based company.

"Our country's very well-positioned on the world stage of specialty coffee. We are recognized as a leading country of origin for specialty coffee."

— FRANCISCO MENA, MANAGING DIRECTOR OF EXCLUSIVE COFFEES IN SAN RAFAEL DE ALAJUELA, COSTA RICA

The long-term relationship partly is about quality, Mena said. "Based on what Scooter's Coffee buys, based on what they pay, it's specialty-grade coffee." Costa Rican coffee is an important part of the overall blend of coffee that Scooter's Coffee customers enjoy.

The relationship also is part of the direct supply chain that co-founders Don and Linda Eckles began early in Scooter's Coffee's history.

Coffee has a high cost of production and it's a commodity, subject to the world trade market's supply and demand swings, Mena said. "Having a direct supply agreement with Harvest Roasting and Scooter's Coffee gives a special identity to the coffee we supply, elevating it above general commodity coffees."

The agreement assures producers that they will be paid more than the cost of production, he said. "We strongly believe in giving the producer value for his coffee based on the quality of the beans, the effort, the cost of production and other factors. We have relationships with farmers all over Costa Rica to provide specialty coffee that we send to Harvest Roasting."

Exclusive Coffees focuses not only on developing "cup quality," Mena said, but also on having a positive impact on the economics of the coffee producers and their families. "We're a local company, 100 percent Costa Rican company, and we understand the culture, the needs and the economics of our people. We understand our identity."

FARMERS EXPECT TO GROW 22.9 BILLION POUNDS OF COFFEE IN 2023.

Costa Rican coffee farmer Jose Ordoñez.

A 1960s law in Costa Rica helps regulate the coffee market so that producers and other parts of the industry can be profitable long-term. "Coffee beans really impact producers if you pay them well, above the cost of production," Mena said. "That's a differentiating factor which makes buyers feel comfortable and trustworthy with Costa Rica, which guarantees sustainability all across the board."

Coffee prices are still influenced by world commodity prices, Mena said. "But more and more we're seeing direct trade relationships like the one with Scooter's Coffee and Harvest Roasting. As long as every member of the supply chain understands their costs and are recognized in a decent way, their margins, their understanding of the whole chain, it works."

Scooter's Coffee visitors, including franchisees Deanna and Mike Braunberger, standing at center, meet with Finca Sumava coffee farm team members, below, Jose Ordoñez, left, Francisco Mena and Johnny Alpizar.

Two or three times a year, officials from Scooter's Coffee and Harvest Roasting come to Costa Rica for "coffee friendship time" and to verify the status of the next crop.

Exclusive Coffees has moved into a new and bigger facility to prepare for the increase in Scooter's Coffee locations. "We're prepared for growth," Mena said. "It's a blessing. We are very thankful and grateful for Scooter's Coffee and Harvest Roasting. It has been a journey of impact on Costa Rica and our families." •

In a world of competitive coffee trade, farmers often lose money on each crop sold. This puts their families and their farms at risk.

Scooter's Coffee buys directly from the farmers and pays above market price.

These proud farmers can invest back into their family farms, their communities, and the environment.

A FEW OF OUR PRODUCTS

Scooter's Coffee expands its product lineup, sometimes at the suggestion of baristas or other team members, but the menu remains relatively stable to maintain service speed and avoid confusion. "It's easy to drift into complexity, and that's what companies do as they get larger," Don said. "We fight that all the time."

Iced Caramelicious
Scooterdoodle Cookies
Maple Waffle Sandwich
Birthday Cake Pop
Spicy Sausage Burrito
Espresso Shot
Brewed Coffee
Caramelicious Muffin
Georgia Peach Iced Tea
Prickly Pear Infusion
Vertigo Smoothie

REAL PIE

Linda's grandmother has a crazy-good pumpkin pie recipe. I was sitting there one day eating a piece of Linda's pumpkin pie. I wondered how a smoothie would taste if you used real pumpkin pie instead of pumpkin syrup or pumpkin sauce like everybody else does. I just threw a hunk of pumpkin pie in there and it was so good. We started baking pumpkin pie without the crust and using that in smoothies.

— DON ECKLES

CHAPTER 11

A NEW EXECUTIVE TEAM
BUFFETT OFFERS ADVICE

IN 2015 I WROTE Warren Buffett a letter and asked him to buy us.

The reason was, I was 60 years old and I didn't want to leave the business, but I loved the way Berkshire Hathaway (Buffett's investment company) handles things. They buy companies, but you continue to run that company — make money, but you run your company, and they hold companies for a long time, sometimes forever.

He was very kind. He wrote back to me for more information, and I wrote him a long letter telling how our model works and why it would be the investment of a lifetime for him.

I told him we had maybe 100 stores, that nobody's doing what we do other than a couple of small places, and with him investing in us we could get really serious about building a lot of stores fast and we could really become big.

At the time we had a valuation that said we were worth between $38 million and $70 million. We'd want to be on the higher side of that, but I said, for him we would take less because we would really like to be a Berkshire company.

He wrote a nice letter back and said we were too small to "move the needle" at Berkshire. I tell people all the time, I'm one of the few people in the world who has a rejection letter from Warren Buffett.

But I still hope that the day will come when he'll say, "Yeah, we'll do it."

In the exchange of letters, Mr. Buffett suggested that we talk to McCarthy Capital, an Omaha-based investment firm. Soon after, Patrick Duffy, president and managing partner of McCarthy Capital, reached out to us.

Our partnership with McCarthy Capital has been a blessing also. Patrick and Matt Breunsbach (managing director) have been valued partners for several years. They helped us think big a lot of times. Sometimes they helped us not think quite so big, but they've been really good partners.

Edge Magazine, February 2015:

Warren Buffett suggested contacting McCarthy Capital.

Omaha World-Herald, May 11, 2015:

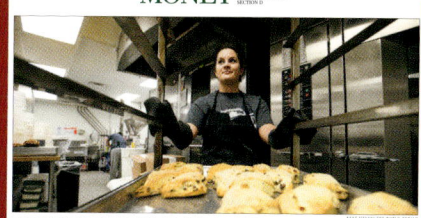

Scooter's way beyond its mom-and-pop shop days

Scooters: Headquarters expansion will be accomplished in phases

BERKSHIRE HATHAWAY INC.
1440 KIEWIT PLAZA
OMAHA, NEBRASKA 68131
TELEPHONE (402) 346-1400
FAX (402) 346-0476

WARREN E. BUFFETT, CHAIRMAN

May 21, 2015

Mr. Don Eckles
Founder/CEO
Boundless Enterprises LLC
6824 J Street
Omaha, NE 68117

Dear Don:

I haven't known much about the coffee business so thanks for the education. You write an interesting letter.

Why don't you send me your last audit as well as any interim financials so that I can have a better insight as to the economics of the business. And let me know what you would like to do – the more specific about valuation, equity percentages, etc. the better. I get so many proposals that I like to find out whether I'm on the same page with people before spending a lot of time thinking further.

Whatever the outcome, I wish you the best.

Sincerely,

Warren E. Buffett

WEB/db

6-1-15

Don –

You have done a terrific job in building a business & your explanation of it to me was clear & logical.

However, it just doesn't fit what I am trying to do at Berkshire. Moving the needle on a 350 billion market cap is daunting.

One possibility for you might be McCarthy & Co. It's local, well-capitalized & your size fits them.

In any event, I wish you & Linda the best. What you have already accomplished is admirable & I know there is more to come. – Warren

OUTSIDE INVESTORS

"At the time, the company was even too small for us," Patrick Duffy said. "It was still entrepreneurial and not quite ready for an institutional investor. But we really liked Don, and he's very charming and persuasive, so we gave him some advice."

Among the suggestions Don heeded: He moved to a support role as chairman and co-founder while Todd Graeve became CEO and assumed day-to-day operations. "Todd started growing as a CEO, building a team and making more institutional-scale decisions," Patrick said. "They circulated back to us a few years later. We made our investment in the spring of 2018. It's been a really good partnership — great people, great company, terrific growth outlook.

Patrick Duffy, president and managing partner of McCarthy Capital and a board member of Boundless Enterprises.

"There's tremendous opportunity to continue its growth trajectory and velocitize the opening of new stores, from 20 or 30 a year to hundreds. To be able to execute those opportunities is going to require continued investment in talent and infrastructure. We'll need talent that's done it in a rapidly growing enterprise before, and has particular energy and expertise that can help in this transition to a large-scale organization."

McCarthy's sources of capital include pension funds, insurance companies and wealthy families and individuals. The 27 percent ownership of Scooter's Coffee is one of 13 portfolio investments by McCarthy Capital Fund VI.

"Our investors entrust us to make investments in smaller private companies, get engaged with those companies and add value to their opportunities and strategies," said Patrick, now a board member of Boundless Enterprises, the holding company of Scooter's Coffee.

From those investors, he said, "we get a lot of positive commentary on our activities, including Scooter's Coffee, especially from local investors who see a lot of Scooter's Coffee locations. The investment is performing well and people like being part of a success story.

"We're particularly proud of being part of this growth story in our hometown. That gives us a lot of comfort and meaning and satisfaction in our work.

"It really is an amazing Omaha success story, and no doubt it's possible because we've got the right business climate here and the kind of talent to be able to do it. Don and Linda are remarkable entrepreneurs. Going from today's $400 million a year in system-wide sales to $800 million, we'll have plenty of challenges. But they won't be as difficult and as fragile as it was from zero to the first $400 million."

Any changes in Scooter's Coffee investments are far in the future, Patrick said. "We're just focused on helping the company capture the growth opportunity, and for the most part, that's expansion of the number of units that are open. The company has a stockpile of commitments from franchisees and prospective franchisees to open new stores. Moving those commitments through the pipeline and getting those doors open is the big opportunity for everybody.

"There's tremendous upside over the next five or 10 years as they continue to execute this plan. We're very excited about it." •

SENIOR MANAGEMENT TEAM

TODD GRAEVE, CEO

Todd, who grew up in the Omaha area, was working as a chief financial officer in Titusville, Florida, when his sister, Tracy Bouwens, made an offer: Would he join her and her husband, former pro football player Shawn Bouwens, in a franchise to open 50 Scooter's Coffee stores in the Kansas City area?

Todd agreed and, without realizing it at the time, took the first step toward becoming the top executive at Scooter's Coffee.

A graduate of Yutan, Nebraska, High School, Todd earned a business degree from the University of Nebraska-Lincoln and became a certified public accountant, working eight years with an Omaha accounting firm before one of its clients offered him the Florida job.

Joining the Bouwens in 2005, Todd was a hands-on partner in Kansas City, sometimes making drinks alongside the baristas besides handling real estate transactions, finances and related duties. "I learned operations from Tracy and Shawn and also went through the training systems that Scooter's Coffee offers."

Todd already had a family connection to the coffee company: His father, Keith Graeve, was an early investor. In 2008, Todd moved to Omaha to became chief financial officer at Scooter's Coffee at co-founder Don Eckles' invitation.

"After relocating to Omaha, I began to work more directly with Scooter's leaders including Don," Todd said. "Don and I began to merge as business partners, seeing business and the world through the same filters and aligning mindset toward franchisee success. We became partners in a vision to build something very special, and that developed into a deep friendship today."

When Don expanded the executive team in 2016, Todd became chief executive officer, with Don remaining as chairman.

Todd and his wife, Melanie, have daughters Mackenzie and Madison. Along with Mackenzie's husband, Jacob Burnett, the family has ownership in a 22-store Scooter's Coffee franchise in the Midwest and plan to build more.

"When the sun sets on our roles with the company one day, I'd like for my friendship with Don to remain close along with our families," Todd said. "I'm still a relatively young guy, but the time will come when there will be new leaders. That leadership transition would have to be evident, and it would have to be right for our employees and franchisees." •

"You need to reach a certain size, maybe a couple hundred stores, to really test the viability of the boat you're in. Did we properly scale ahead? Can we support the growing weight of the company into the future? An enterprise aspiring for growth must resource and strategize well ahead of the curve."

— TODD GRAEVE, CEO

JOE THORNTON, PRESIDENT

On March 30, 2022, Lacey Navarrete, corporate recruiter for Scooter's Coffee, phoned Joe to introduce a new career opportunity: becoming the first-ever president at Scooter's Coffee.

After discussing the job and the company, Lacey asked the fateful question: "Are you willing to move to Omaha?"

"You could almost feel her bracing for impact, expecting the answer to be 'no,'" Joe said. "But I responded with an enthusiastic 'yes!'"

He accepted the job and, shortly after he arrived in Omaha in June 2022, Joe was in a meeting with co-founder Don Eckles and CEO Todd Graeve. Don mentioned that he doubted Joe would have answered Lacey's call a few years ago when the company was much smaller.

Joe said, "Actually, I might have taken the call. What attracted me was that the call was not from an executive recruiter. It was Lacey, an internal recruiter, reaching out about this job opportunity. I interpreted that as a signal that the organization didn't want their message, especially their message of culture, to get lost in translation through an executive recruiter."

In a career spanning nearly 40 years, Joe worked for Blockbuster Video during its high growth years, then Starbucks during its high growth years and, most recently, held COO posts at Jamba Juice and HMSHost, helping each of them turn around their business model due to loss of market share and pandemic recovery, respectively.

With Joe's coffee experience and his deep understanding of drive-thru as he oversaw the national drive-thru team at Starbucks, and with his experience scaling companies, Joe was the right person at the right time.

"The promise of Scooter's Coffee is unlike anything I've seen before," he said.

"This just feels different from all other companies I have worked for. This company embraces its values — Integrity, LOVE, Humility, and Courage — in a way that I haven't seen before. It's the simplest, yet strongest set of values that exists, making this culture incredibly strong."

Another reason Joe agreed to the move: He had made three business trips to Omaha over the years, including a trip to help open a Starbucks location in Creighton University's student commons area.

"The window of opportunity is real. Our growth opportunity is as high as we'd like it to be, but we want to be very careful about how we grow and protect our values."

— JOE THORNTON, PRESIDENT

SCOOTER'S COFFEE SENIOR MANAGEMENT TEAM

BILL BLACK
Chief Marketing Officer

RICHARD HEYMAN
Chief Strategy Officer

DAVE ANDERSON
Chief Legal Officer

GREG HAND
Chief Financial Officer

KIM ELLIS
Chief Development Officer

MISSY MCKINLEY
Senior Vice President, **Operations**

NICK JARECKE
Senior Vice President, Supply Chain

MIKALA FRIEDRICH
Vice President, Human Resources

"Out of the hundreds of stores I've opened, that one stood out for me because there was a story to be told — taking bricks from the original pathway of the university and infusing them into the Starbucks design. It was brilliant. And, of course, everyone was incredibly kind all the times I visited Omaha.

"Also, you don't find franchise systems that are this family-centric," Joe said. "It's been that way from the start." Many other franchise companies expand through large, highly leveraged franchisees already operating many different brands. By contrast, many of the early franchisees were connected to Don and Linda in some way along their life journey.

"What I also love about this model is that we are opening in small towns, where it's the fireman, the teacher, the physical therapist who are putting their money into opening a store," he said. "It's not a part-time focus. This is their focus, and it shows up when they open a store and the community embraces the new location and that person as an owner.

"Scooter's Coffee doesn't reject the idea of large franchise owners, but we don't want to do anything that fractures our culture. We don't want people in this business model if their hearts aren't in it."

The result is strong organic growth by owners who started with one store and then opened another and another. "It's incredibly exciting."

When Joe arrived, he and Todd divided the top executive duties. The humility by which Don and Todd both operate has been striking and a true leadership example to follow, Joe said. Both Don and Todd have repeatedly stated, "The business was built with grit, but grit will not sustain us as we grow bigger." They went on to say, "We're going into a different season of the business, with big aspirations, and we need help doing it."

It was a clear sign of incredibly humble leaders, Joe said. "You don't often get people at the top of the organization who will say those things out loud." Scooter's Coffee now has a full leadership team structure in place and poised for growth.

Joe was born in Kentucky and lived in Texas most of his life. He and his wife, Inez, moved into their new Omaha home. "My wife said Omaha felt like home from day one, the house and the city both.

"I believe there is just something about Omaha, just like there is just something about Scooter's Coffee. If you can just get people to visit, I think people will feel differently." •

President Joe Thornton talks with employees at the new headquarters.

CHAPTER 12

ZIG-ZAGGING
LEARNING FROM BUSINESS PHILOSOPHERS

I LOVED ZIG ZIGLAR'S stories. Zig was a motivational speaker and writer who was able to put very important concepts into a phrase or sentence. Three of those that I have always remembered are:

"THE MAJOR DIFFERENCE BETWEEN THE BIG SHOT AND THE LITTLE SHOT IS THE BIG SHOT IS JUST A LITTLE SHOT WHO KEPT ON SHOOTING."

This speaks to persistence. I'm paraphrasing now, but he goes on to point out that many people who tried but gave up had no idea how close they may have been to success. There's an old saying that says, if it was easy, everyone would do it.

The truth is, it's not easy. Success is rarely found overnight. It takes hard work, persistence, some smarts and sometimes even a little luck. The only sure way to not succeed is to give up, or not try in the first place.

When we first decided to move back to my hometown and start Scooter's Coffee, we were in the coffee business, living in California. I contacted a commercial real estate agent in Omaha to help me find our first site. We started this process a year or so before we moved back so we'd have plenty of time to find the right location.

I flew back to Omaha a time or two to look at locations with him. We drove the market together and talked about the model and what we were looking for. We knew it would be tough finding that first landlord who would agree to let us build a little building in their parking lot and sell coffee. In the mid-1990s, very few people were doing that.

300th location grand opening, Oklahoma City, Okla., January 2021.

SURPRISINGLY GOOD

A lot of folks get in tentatively. They'll get into a franchise and buy one or two stores and keep doing other businesses or keep their jobs. It's surprising how many of them quickly sell their other business or quit their jobs and focus on Scooter's Coffee. It's a good business.

— DON ECKLES

The agent really tried but had very little success. He worked at it for months, but one day called and said, "You need to find someone else. I just can't do it." I encouraged him not to give up, that we would get there, and once we did, it would get easier to find sites. He agreed to keep trying. Eventually, he just stopped returning my calls. I didn't blame him. Real estate agents make money by getting deals done. No deal, no money. I get it.

I eventually found that first site on my own. Then the second, and so on. Eventually, I partnered with another real estate person who went on to do close to a hundred or so deals for us.

One day I was in my agent's office talking about sites. As I left the building I was in the elevator with someone who looked familiar. I said, "You look familiar, do we know each other? I'm Don Eckles." It was my former real estate agent, who told me, "Don, you are the biggest professional mistake I've ever made. I tell this story to my young agents to remind them to never give up on a deal."

"FOR 40 HOURS A WEEK COMPETITION IS AWFULLY STIFF BUT AFTER THAT THERE'S VERY LITTLE COMPETITION."

I think about this all the time. Zig spoke to the idea that if you want more, you need to do more. And the point of this saying, at least what I took from it, is that everyone does what they have to do. That's just called making a living. If you want more, you need to do more than what others are willing to do.

You don't even have to do that much more to start seeing some results. Everybody works 40 hours a week, in theory. Doing more than that, more than what's needed, will lead to better results. For example, working 10 percent more is only four more hours a week, but those four hours compounding on top of each other eventually lead to noticeable results.

If you want to have nice things in life, you have to work harder than the folks who are happy to just get by. Everyone has to do the minimum. It's doing more than the minimum that will start to pay dividends.

400th location grand opening, Katy, Texas, April 2022.

"YOUR ATTITUDE, NOT YOUR APTITUDE, WILL DETERMINE YOUR ALTITUDE."

Years ago, a couple of business partners and I had an opportunity to purchase a business that was doing okay but had very strong potential. The partners didn't want to do that. We were doing fine as we were, and they just didn't want to take the risk. The more I tried to convince them, the more they dug in their heels. Finally, I said, "Guys, I'm buying the business, whether you join me or not."

One of them said, "Don, you have to understand that you're a glass half-full guy, and I'm a glass half-empty guy." The other guy said, "Yeah, and I'm a *Hey, where's my glass?* guy." They both eventually joined me in the venture and it worked out well.

I honestly don't know if I was just born an optimist, or if it was a developed mindset. Maybe a little of both. But I really don't understand, and have little tolerance for, negative attitudes. It just seems so self-defeating to me. "If you think you can, or you think you can't, you're right." I don't know who came up with that, but I believe it. Attitude is everything. •

> "We'll be the second-largest specialty coffee company in the country by 2023."
>
> — DON ECKLES

500th location grand opening, in Orlando, Fla., December 2022.

DON ECKLES: IN WHICH WAYS CAN WE?

I once worked for a guy by the name of Ron Kreie who would often use an acronym he probably borrowed: IWWCW, which stands for "in which ways can we?"

Ron took me under his wing and mentored me. He wasn't above raising his voice several decibel levels and making not-so-veiled threats. His work ethic and the IWWCW concept have stayed with me forever.

Don with J.T.'s General Store executives Gary Brown, left, and Ron Kreie, right, in 1986.

Ron didn't want to hear why we couldn't accomplish something. He started with the idea that most things CAN be accomplished, even if they're hard or seem improbable or even impossible. IWWCW reminds you to focus on the things that need to happen to accomplish a goal, rather than focusing on the goal itself.

For example, our business model has always worked well at lower and middle volumes, but in 2019 we realized that we could raise our volumes dramatically if we could get everyone on the same page on a goal of $1 million average unit volume by the end of 2024 — a BHAG, or big, hairy, audacious goal.

Following the IWWCW concept, we focused on things that would impact the financial results to move toward that BHAG. That includes being faster (work on speed), getting better store sites (new approach to real estate), selling more to each customer (work on up-selling and new products), and getting new customers (telling people why to choose Scooter's Coffee).

We focused on the process instead of the result.

IWWCW is a powerfully positive approach: nothing is impossible. It may not be easy and you may not accomplish everything you want, but it gives you the opportunity if you're willing to put in the time and pay the price. •

LESSONS LEARNED

An idea I didn't originate is IWWCW — in which ways can we? Don't tell me why it can't be done. Tell me what we need to get it done, and let's do that.

Most things can be figured out if you stop and think about what it is you're really trying to do, what are you really trying to accomplish? Don't focus on the end result. Focus on the stuff that you need to get to the end result.

BIG, HAIRY, AUDACIOUS GOALS

In "Built to Last," author Jim Collins says great companies set "big, hairy, audacious goals," or BHAGs.

Todd Graeve, chief executive officer of Scooter's Coffee, said executives held an off-site meeting in 2018 and began dreaming about BHAGs. "How far could we go? What are the possibilities if we think big?"

One person suggested growing from about 150 stores to 500, making Scooter's Coffee No. 2 in the industry behind Starbucks. "Pretty big thinking," Todd said. "Someone piped in and said, 'Let's do that in a decade,' and somebody said, 'What if we do 500 stores in five years?' Remember, it took us 20 years to get to 150 stores.

"That was audacious, but it wasn't hairy enough," Todd said. "And somebody said, 'What about 1,000 stores in five years?' The room went quiet. And we thought, 1,000 stores in five years — is that even possible? Could we do that? And so we cast it — 1,000 stores by the beginning of 2024."

The idea spread within the company and among franchisees and investors, and some doubts surfaced. "You could almost see a collective eye-roll," Todd said. "It took 20 years to get to 150 stores. Really? You're going to build to 1,000 stores in five years flat? The answer: Yes, that's what we're going to do.

"The beautiful thing about a BHAG is, it gives you permissions to resource differently. You can create the road map — open 35 stores the first year, then 70 the next, then 135 the next. We'll ladder up to 1,000 stores.

"We began to resource proactively. We began to measure differently. We knew that to accelerate and elevate, we'd need to surround ourselves with talented and skilled leaders who have done this before.

"Today, the die is cast. We're going to surpass 1,000 stores by mid-2024, slightly after the original goal. Now, we're dreaming again. Could we grow to 5,000 stores domestically? How about international expansion? Could we be a multi-national company and do it well? We believe the answer is absolutely yes, so long as we never compromise our Core Values of Integrity, LOVE, Humility and Courage."

The next BHAG awaits. •

DRIVING INNOVATION

Todd Graeve cited a study on how pre-school children, playing within fenced playgrounds, tend to explore more freely than children on playgrounds without fences.

"There is an interesting translation to business and innovation," Todd said. "Fences can be good. They more clearly define parameters for growth, such as integrity as a core value or speed of service as a key competency. If we establish fences, we encourage exploration that drives incremental value within the right parameters. Can we innovate for faster drive-thru lanes, for example? Innovation within established fences allows for focused work and compounding value while staying true to who we are."

SUCCESS TAKES TIME, BUT NOT FOREVER

Business Never Stands Still. You're Either Moving Forward or Backward

a. Too often when we buy a business, we work really hard at learning to make the drinks right and how to staff the store. We're working extra hours learning how to use QuickBooks and when to make a Sam's Club run. We might even spend some time trying to get to know our customers.

b. When exhaustion sets in, most of us will settle into our business and try to figure out how to make it work. We've got the business under control (for the most part), but we're still not making much money.

c. We attend meetings and hope we hear some magical answers to business growth or profitability. Or worse, we give up trying and assume that it's the company's fault.

How Long Is Too Long?

a. If you begin to feel like you've just "bought a job" … you've just bought a job! The danger is when you allow those feelings to take root.

b. Progress should be steady. Whether you're growing quickly or slowly, you should be steadily growing. If you're not, something needs attention, and fast!

c. Constant growth requires constant focus. Your major focus should not be handing drinks out the window. Your major focus should be building your business. That means:

   1. Hiring and training great employees to meet your customers' needs
   2. In-depth knowledge of drink preparation techniques
   3. In-depth knowledge of product quality and consistency
   4. Constant supervision of customer service
   5. Constant supervision of store cleanliness
   6. Supervision of customer service speed
   7. Regular marketing efforts
   8. Facility maintenance and appearance
   9. Knowledge of monthly and ongoing promotions
   10. Knowledge of company policies
   11. Knowledge of company training opportunities
   12. Knowledge of company marketing assistance programs
   13. Knowledge of your store's cost of goods and labor, as well as realistic target goals for both of those categories
   14. Banking, taxes, bill paying, etc.
   15. Knowledge of everything else you should know that I've forgotten to list here

**Good News!
The Magic Answer Is ...
(Insert Your Name Here)**

a. The truth is, it's up to you to make your business successful. We can help you, and support your efforts, but ultimately, you're the one who decides whether you succeed or not.

b. You must develop a mindset of success. "I will do whatever I must do to make my business successful."

c. Your business is no different from anyone else's business. You can either make it successful, or not.

CHAPTER 13

THE FUTURE
PROTECTING OUR CULTURE AND CORE VALUES

I'M ALWAYS THINKING about the franchisees who have invested their money with us and the employees who have said, "Yes, I will spend my career with you." And our investors, by the way, who entrust us with their money, my mom and my father-in-law included. We were going to build warehouses, and they would lend me money and I would give them some Scooter's Coffee stock, which was really worth nothing then. It eventually turned out to be a good thing, but they loaned us money because they loved us and believed in us, not because they thought it would work out really well down the road.

Eastern Iowa franchisee Mark Holtkamp, right, with store manager Kevin Wood in Iowa City.

You have to think about these groups. And so it's not just about somebody coming along and offering a boatload of money. People come along and offer us a boatload of money every day. We're not interested in that.

The important thing is, how do we remain Scooter's Coffee 20 years from now or 30 years from now or 40 years from now? How do we make sure this is a place where our employees can retire from and our franchisees and their families can grow wealth?

We're a family-owned business. But we've got something here that's too big to be just handed over to our kids. People are depending on us to get it just right. We've got a commitment to all these folks.

If a plane falls from the sky with me in it, what happens to Scooter's Coffee and Harvest Roasting? What about all those groups of people? That's when I asked Todd Graeve to be CEO of the company. Even though Todd wasn't an operations guy and had never been a CEO, I always knew Todd would look out for the three groups of people — our investors, our employees, and our franchisees. And he would protect our core values and get the right people. It's worked out exactly like that.

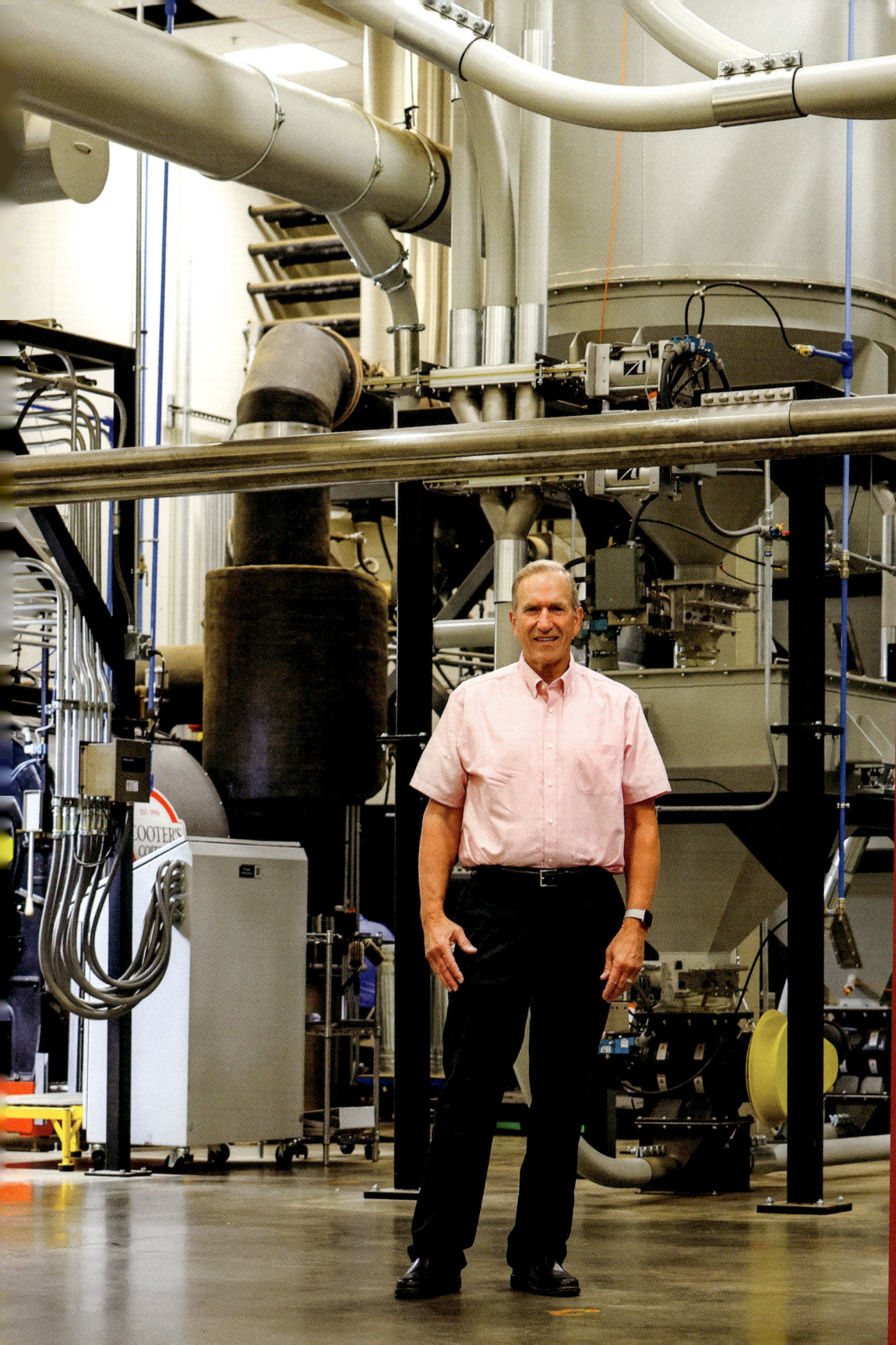

"It's expensive to go into a business. It's a risk, and you're trusting us to get it right. I like our model. I like what we do. I think we're on the right track. Our business is really good."

— DON ECKLES

WE'RE NOT ONLY IN THE COFFEE BUSINESS,

CULTIVATING RELATIONSHIPS

Everything we do is based on the values that we at Scooter's Coffee believe in and live by. The result? A company that recognizes relationships are the foundation of our success, and at the end of the day, relationships are what really matter.

COFFEE FARMERS & THEIR FAMILIES

This is where it all begins, with personal visits, farmer direct trade, and mutual respect. We couldn't be more grateful for our friends located on family farms all over the globe, who grow the Scooter's Coffee specialty graded coffee beans.

FRANCHISE PARTNERS

Franchisees are dear to our hearts. When people choose to own a Scooter's Coffee, they're fully supported every step of the way, with autonomy, guidance and encouragement.

WE'RE IN THE PEOPLE BUSINESS, TOO.

TEAM MEMBERS

Simply put, we like and respect one another. Love, after all, is among our core values. We're the recipients of it, and our aim is to share it, no matter what role we play in the company.

YOU

Customers love Scooter's Coffee not only for our amazing coffee, but also the genuine happiness our baristas share with each other and with customers. We see you and care about you.

Why did we arrange for McCarthy Capital to own 27 percent of the company? Not because we needed the money, but because we were a family-owned business, we'd taken investments from friends and family to build a warehouse and more stores, and we'd given out shares of stock. We were paying out 75 percent of our taxable income as distributions to shareholders. At first it wasn't a real big deal, but you can imagine that after a few years it was a big deal. People were getting nice checks every month.

Suddenly, we've got an opportunity to be the second-largest specialty coffee company in the country fairly quickly. But we're not going to be able to do that if we're giving all of our profits away. We took the investment from McCarthy and distributed that to our investors and said, we're just going to distribute money for taxes every year. The rest of it, we're going to invest.

The way private equity works, there will come a day when McCarthy needs to do something else. We're already thinking about how that looks. Do we buy them back out? Do we go public? Do we circle back around? We're a much larger company now. Within the next couple years we will be a very large and profitable company. This is a good business, and it's going to be a better business two years from now and a better business two years after that and a better business two years after that.

Cafe, March 2021

At any rate, whatever is next is going to be something that's got to fit our values and fit our long-term plan of still being Scooter's Coffee and still being based out of Omaha, Nebraska.

We really love the long-term nature of our business. When we have to decide to partner with somebody other than McCarthy or something else, we want to make decisions in the best long-term interests of everybody involved. •

A NEW HEADQUARTERS

In 2022, Scooter's Coffee moved its headquarters to the top floor of a building in the Miracle Hills Office Park in central Omaha. Besides adding space for the company's growing staff, the move opened up former headquarters offices in the Harvest Roasting production center and warehouse on the city's southwestern edge. Design graphics in the new headquarters emphasize the company's core values, mission and brand promise, and the employee snack bar includes, of course, a full-fledged coffee bar.

"We're super excited about the location, the building and being able to expand our presence in Omaha."

— GREG HAND, CHIEF FINANCIAL OFFICER

HALL OF FAME

OMAHA BUSINESS HALL OF FAME 2022 INDUCTEES

Don Eckles
Co-Founder and Chairman
Scooter's Coffee,
Harvest Roasting

Linda Eckles
Co-Founder
Scooter's Coffee,
Harvest Roasting

John F. Lund
Founder & Chairman
Lund Company

Jay Noddle
President & CEO
Noddle Companies

Carmen Tapio
Chief Executive Officer
North End Teleservices, LLC

When Linda and Don Eckles took the stage at the Omaha Business Hall of Fame dinner and induction ceremony in 2022, she couldn't help thinking about her days as a cheerleader for Culbertson High School in southwestern Nebraska.

"As a cheerleader, I was in front of large groups regularly. And so, while I thought I would be nervous getting on stage in front of so many people, I wasn't really nervous at all. It was a fun evening spent with family and friends."

While Don is an experienced "talker" from his days in radio, Linda carefully rehearsed a few lines. Some friends told her, "Just talk from your heart," and another said, "You have to own it tonight."

"I'm like, 'Oh, okay,'" she said. "That really helped me. This is our time, and just enjoy the evening."

Early in their acceptance speech on a stage in front of hundreds of Omaha's top business leaders, Linda pulled the microphone away from Don's hand and said, "Well, actually, speaking in front of a large group isn't my thing. But my things are my grandkids, my family, hugs and smiley faces."

The crowd laughed, partly because Don seemed so surprised that she had interrupted him. Later, Linda said Don was supposed to put his notes on the lectern and let her say something. Instead he took the microphone and started talking. "I wanted to say something and that's why I took the mic from him. It really was not planned."

Don's comments included a description of his going broke in his early businesses, and some in the audience laughed a little uncomfortably. "I guess that's a lesson that quite a few of us had learned," he said later. "People just don't say that out loud very often. They don't say that business is hard. You work and you try to find a way and you don't find it, and you try again and you don't find it again. You just keep doing it."

Standing, from left: Lauren, Tyler, Traci and Eric Gabriel; Bailey Kipper, Linda Eckles, Bill Kipper, Don Eckles, Sydney and Dustin Kipper. Seated, from left: Juli Kipper, Nathan Gabriel, Ellie, Chandra, Aubrey and Mason Kipper.

In his speech, Don praised the company's leadership team and franchisees. With a tear in her eye, Linda said directly to the tables of company team members, "They really are family to us. And we're so grateful for you."

Best of all, Linda said later, "The grandchildren were proud of us. One granddaughter cried through the whole thing. They were just hugging on me. They loved being dressed up and looking good. And Don's mom was there. That was special, too. It was just a great evening." •

SCOOTER'S COFFEE TIMELINE

1998
- March 23, 1998: Scooter's Java Express opens in Bellevue, NE.
- Caramelicious is introduced after a barista request, eventually becoming our signature drink.

2000
- Harvest Roasting is formed.

2002
- Don and Linda host the first franchising meeting, at a Holiday Inn in Omaha.

2004
- The second store moves to 72nd and Dodge, Omaha's premier intersection. Four others also open in Omaha.

2006
- Named Emerging Business of the Year by the Greater Omaha Chamber of Commerce.
- Scooter's Coffee becomes one of the first to offer Cold Brew.

1999
- Espresso Blenders, using fresh espresso, joins the menu.
- Second store opens at 72nd and Farnam.
- Don buys a coffee roaster, the first step toward a supply chain.

2001
- Franchising begins; there are five Scooter's Java Express locations.

2003
- The name evolves to Scooter's Coffeehouse.

- A Lincoln barista suggests a new drink: the Red Bull Vertigo Smoothie.

2005
- Todd Graeve joins family members in a Kansas City franchise.

2008
- Todd Graeve named chief financial officer.
- Happy 10th Birthday!

2011
- The name is shortened to Scooter's Coffee.

2014
- 100th store opens.

2016
- Don remains chairman, Todd Graeve is named CEO.

2019
- Scooter's Coffee acquires Crane Coffee.

2022
- Joe Thornton joins Scooter's Coffee as president.
- 400th location opens in Katy, Texas.
- 500th location opens in Orlando, Florida.
- Don & Linda inducted into Omaha Business Hall of Fame.

2012
- Scooter's Coffee bakes cinnamon rolls from scratch at our Omaha headquarters.

2015
- Don offers to sell Scooter's Coffee to Warren Buffett, who declines but offers advice.

2018

- McCarthy Capital acquires 27 percent ownership; Patrick Duffy becomes board member; family shareholders bought out.
- Happy 20th Birthday!

2021
- 300th location opens in Oklahoma City.
- Harvest Roasting delivers milk and water to ice-storm battered areas of Texas.

2023
- 600th-900th locations open.
- Scooter's Coffee becomes the second-largest specialty coffee company in the nation.
- Happy 25th Birthday!

SCOOTER'S COFFEE 25TH BIRTHDAY

Turning 25 is a landmark for any business, but Scooter's Coffee's quarter-century birthday marks just the start. Our birthday celebration comes as the company heads for 1,000 stores soon, with thousands more targeted by new and veteran franchise holders in a growing number of states. For our customers, that means more chances to hear a smiling team member say, "Welcome to Scooter's Coffee. What can we get started for you?"

From left: Dustin, Chandra and Bill Kipper, Linda and Don Eckles, Traci and Eric Gabriel.

Family and longtime team members, from left: Eric Gabriel, Jon Mehuron, Dustin Kipper, Don and Linda, Josi Orsi, Amber Middleton, Bill Kipper and Erin Kastens.

INDEX

A&W Restaurant, 32-33

Alpizar, Johnny, 101

Always Espresso, 47

Anderson, Dave, 112

Baldwin, Chris, 91

Be Amazing Day, 17, 30, 70-71, 75, 77, 139

Big, hairy, audacious goals, 121

Black, Bill, 87, 112

Boundless Enterprises, 65, 106

Bouwens, Tracy and Shawn, 68, 108

Braunberger, Deanna and Mike, 101

Breunsbach, Matt, 104

Brown, Gary, 120

Brown Institute of Broadcasting, 24-25, 27, 141

Buffett, Warren, 104-105, 135

Burnett, Mackenzie and Jacob, 108

Butcher, Susan, 35

Calderon Castillo family, 96

Collins, Jim, 61, 121

Combs, Ward, 33

Crane Coffee, 54-55, 135

Crummer, Kelly, 139

Duffy, Patrick, 104, 106, 135

Eckles, Don: First store, 5; lessons to learn, 16; Be Amazing, 17; early days, 22-26; meets Linda, 26; Presto-X, laundromat, cafe, 30-33; Alaska, Iditarod, Kodiak, 34-39; radio failure, J.T.'s General Store, 41; California and coffee, 42-44; Sweet Things & Java, 45; drive-thru kiosk, 48; returns to Omaha, 50; Scooter's Java Express, 51; "Scooter's," 53; Crane Coffee, 54; customer service, 56; sells Scooter's Coffee, 65; franchising, 68; Immersion, 71; the Good Life, 76; good deeds, 86; Harvest Roasting, 88; Warren Buffett, 104; new CEO, 106; hires president, 110; Zig Ziglar, 114-119; success, 122; future, 124; Hall of Fame, 132

Eckles, Linda: First store, 5; coffee cart, 16; Be Amazing, 17; early days, 26-33; Bomb-Pops, 31; studies business in Anchorage, 34; tracks Don's dogsled, 36; dentist job, 38; California, 42-44; basket of muffins, 46; normal people, 47; Grandmother's, 50; Scooter's Java Express, 51; smiley face stickers, 57; log books, 62-63; Hall of Fame, 132; with Sugar, 144

Eckles, Wayne and Myrna, 23, 40, 48, 89

Eiseley, Loren, 86

Ellis, Kim, 112

Exclusive Coffees, 96-101

Folsom, John, 87

Fox, Eric & Jim, 24, 32

Friedrich, Mikala, 112

Gabriel, Eric, 72, 133, 136, 137

Gabriel, Traci Eckles, 34, 39, 41, 45, 53, 76, 78, 133, 136, back cover

Gabriel, Lauren, Nathan and Tyler, 133, 140, 141

Goad, Josh, 90

Graeve, Keith and Linda, 55, 108

Graeve, Todd: future CEO, 55; joins franchise, 68, 70; franchising is hard work, 74; becomes CEO, 106-109; dividing duties, 110, 112; BHAGs, 121; future, 124, 134

Grow franchise conference, 78

Hammerstrom, Steve and Paulette, 54-55

Hand, Greg, 112, 130

Harvest Roasting, 65, 88-101, 124, 129, 132, 134

Hatoo, Ba, 91

Herman's Nut House, 50

Heyman, Richard, 112

Holtkamp, Mark, 124

Iditarod, 34-37

Jarecke, Nick, 92-93, 112

Java Detour, 48

Jensen, Brooke, 70, 77

J.T.'s General Store, 41-43, 120

Kastens, Erin, 137

Kipper, Bailey, 57, 133, 140, 141

Kipper, Bill, 72, 76, 133, 136, 137

Kipper, Chandra Eckles, 31, 34, 41, 45, 52, 53, 70, 75, 76, 78, 133, 136, back cover

Kipper, Dustin, 72, 133, 136, 137, 140, 141

Kipper, Juli, Ellie, Sydney and Aubrey, 133

Kipper, Mason, 133, 140, 141

Koterba, Jeff, 107

Kreie, Ron, 120

Lampe, Ray, 23

Lee, Yu, 94

Mallow, Melissa, 76

McCarthy Capital, 104-107, 127, 135

McCauley, Kate, 87

McKinley, Missy, 112

Mehuron, Jon, 137

Melonis, Ted, 23

Mena, Francisco, 96-101

Metcalf, Jason, Nancy and Rita, 80-81

Meyers, Joe, 91

Middleton, Amber, 137

Mu, Paw, 94

Mulhern, Liz, 76

Munson, Dale, 24

Navarrete, Lacey, 110

Ordoñez, Jose, 100, 101

Orsi, Josi, 137

Osborne, Tom, 84

Owner Immersion, 71-72

Pavelka, Kent, 40

Podolak, Ed, 23

Radio stations, 24, 27, 32, 34, 37, 40

Redington, Joe, 35

Rynders, Brenda, 68

Spaeth, Stacy Peterson, 52

Sweazy, Austin, 95

Sweet Things & Java, 16, 44-47

Talley, Harold and Maxine, 28, 48

Thornton, Joe, 71, 87, 110-113, 135, 139

Thrasher, Carole and Gary, 51

Wah, Wah, 94

Williams, Chuck, 57

Wood, Kevin, 124

Wounded Warriors, 87

Young, Julian and Brittany, 82-85

Ziglar, Zig, 114-119

ALIGNED HEARTS

"We want to make sure your head and heart are aligned today."

— KELLY CRUMMER, SENIOR DIRECTOR FOR FRANCHISE RECRUITMENT, DURING BE AMAZING DAY

FREE DRINKS!

Stores hold free-drink appreciation days for teachers, health care workers and veterans and offer seasonal menu items to keep things fresh. Scooter's Coffee's web site hosts trivia games, playlists, movie lists and coffee-focused blogs.

$1 MILLION

"We opened a year ago with a 3.0 store design, 638 square feet. We hit $1 million in sales in 237 days open. We're looking at a second location in a nearby town."

— ALABAMA FRANCHISEE

DAGGER TO THE HEART

A longtime customer once told Don that he skipped his daily stop at Scooter's Coffee because the line of cars looked too long. "A dagger in my heart," Don said. "You don't know how much you lose if the line looks too long."

EXTRA SMILES

LEGACY

A former high school biology teacher was looking for something different, saw a Scooter's Coffee shop in Missouri's Ozarks and became a franchisee. "Super-appealing," she said. "I want something for our family, a legacy that lasts beyond us."

LOTSA JOE

Scooter's Coffee opened a store in McCook, Nebraska, and people thought it would kill a local coffee shop named Joltin' Jo's. But both locations are doing well, Don said.

CHANGES

When competitors "re-tool" their operations by adding menu items, changing drive-thru systems and initiating other changes, President Joe Thornton said, "That's an opportunity for growth for us."

JUST A SECOND

What's the value of 1 second? When 100 people per hour go through the line, that's 100 seconds per hour, 13 minutes a day with a potential revenue of $100, or $35,000 a year.

GRANDCHILDREN LEND A HAND

Lauren Gabriel, above, and Bailey Kipper greet customers at drive-thru windows.

Helping at Harvest Roasting are Nathan Gabriel, left, Dustin and Mason Kipper and Tyler Gabriel.

JOURNEY TO AMAZING

25 YEARS OF BUILDING SCOOTER'S COFFEE

BY DON ECKLES

Don and Linda Eckles founded Scooter's Coffee in 1998 in Bellevue, Nebraska, the most successful in a series of businesses they have owned or started since the 1970s. Don, an Omaha native, is a graduate of Omaha Westside High School and the Brown Institute of Broadcasting. Linda is from Culbertson, Nebraska, and a graduate of Culbertson High School, and studied business at Anchorage Community College. They have two daughters, six grandchildren and three great-grandchildren and live in the Omaha area.

Grandchildren today, front to back, Bailey Kipper, Lauren Gabriel, Mason Kipper, Tyler Gabriel, Dustin Kipper and Nathan Gabriel.

EDITOR AND REPORTER
Steve Jordon

DESIGNER
Christine Zueck-Watkins

COPY EDITORS
Mike Holmes
Pam Thomas

PHOTOGRAPHY & IMAGES
Eckles family
Steve Jordon
Jeff Koterba
Ariel Panowicz
Christine Zueck-Watkins

GUIDANCE
Todd Graeve, Joe Thornton and Bill Black of Scooter's Coffee
Joan Lukas of Lukas Partners

SCOOTER'S COFFEE TEAM MEMBERS
Mary Allen
Jasmine Briggins
Kelly Crummer
Ecliserio Delgadillo
Scott Eastman
Dan Forslund
Laurie Kobza
Missy McKinley
Kevin Mosher
Matt Noa
Michelle Pachunka
Jennifer Van Haitsma

"One time I had a customer who was having a really bad day, so I put extra stickers on his cup, and he said, 'Oh, my gosh. Is that a secret code for decaf?' I said, 'No, it's just because I want you to have an extra happy day. I can tell you're having struggles today.'

"We actually just pinch ourselves. It's the people we have with us that help make this happen. It's not us. I just want to keep enjoying this journey of what we're doing."

— LINDA ECKLES

25 YEARS OF SHARING THE LOVE.

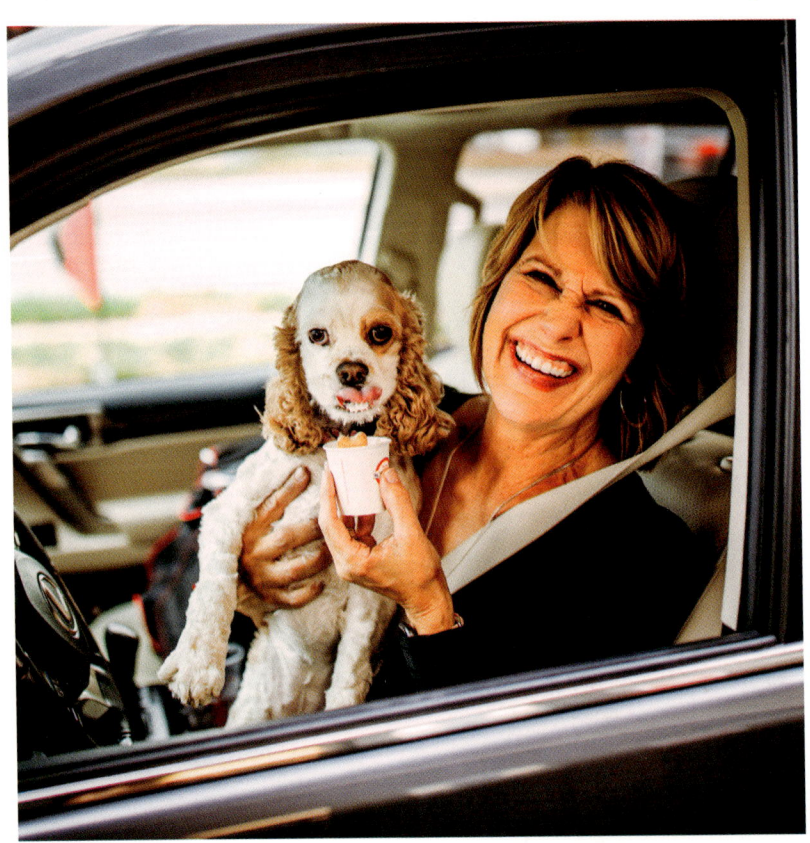

 "SUGAR IS MY NAME. PUP CUPS ARE MY GAME."

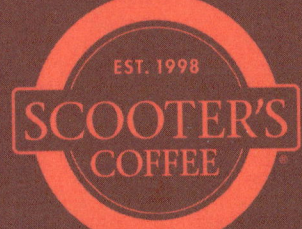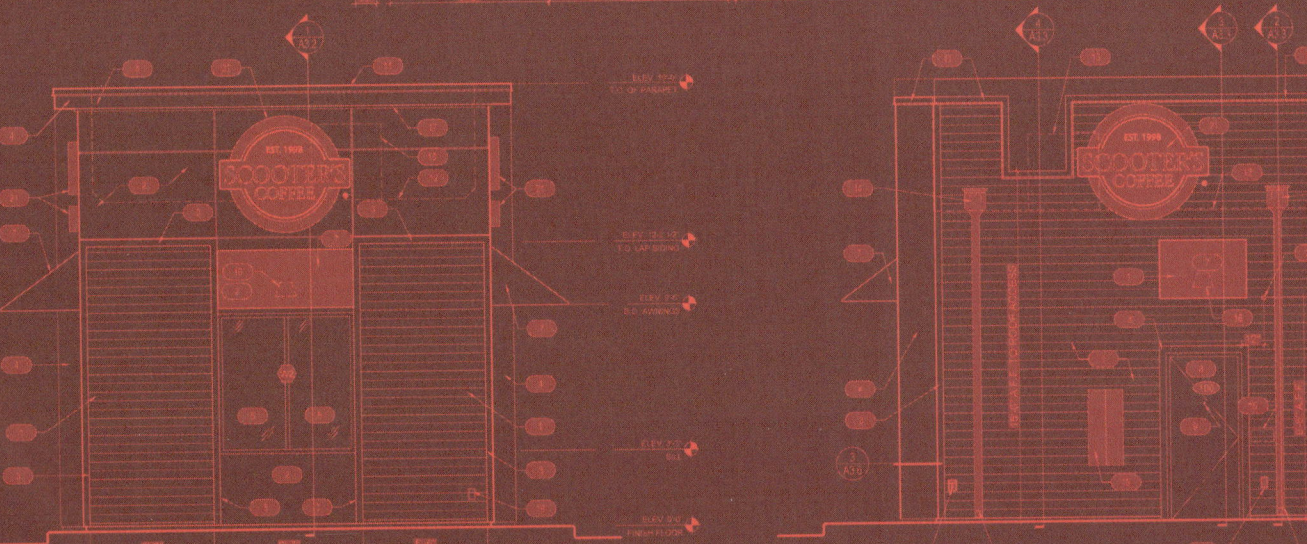